My Father, My Hero

Becoming Your Child's Best Friend

Terry Olsen

Published by
WinePress Publishing
MOUNTLAKE TERRACE, WA 98043

The Lord bless you and give you His Peace

Terry Olsen

Printed in the Canada on recycled paper.

ISBN 1-883893-13-5

This book is dedicated to....

My wife, Mardi....
A person of wisdom and caring.

John & Megen....
Two wonderful people with whom I was
priviledged
to share "the growing years."

Heidi
A step-daughter I have come to love.

MY FATHER, MY HERO
Becoming Your Child's Best Friend
by Terry Olsen

TABLE OF CONTENTS

Acknowledgments

This is a book about fathers, and also a book about friendships. Over the years many friends have contributed to my life and to the experiences which form the basis for this book. These friends have helped me through difficult, but rewarding, times. My genuine appreciation and thanksgiving is offered to each one.

First of all, I want to thank my wife, Mardi, for the wonderful encouragement she has afforded me in this project. I have come to value her keen insights into relationships in everyday life.

A special thank-you to my two biological children, John and Megen. Day in and day out, they endured my attempts at single parenting. It is they who helped me re-define "family."

Thank you to my step-daughter, Heidi, who helped me understand what a blended family is all about.

I also offer my thanks to John and Megen's birth mother, who was an excellent parent during those early, formative years.

I am blessed to have a mother like mine. Allee helped me understand the word, optimism, no matter what the circumstances. Her truly cheerful heart was the best medicine of all.

Special thanks to the following:

—To my father, Louis, for being our provider growing-up.

—To my two brothers, Tom and George, who have been there for me, especially during the difficult times.

—To my early spiritual mentors, Mike McCutcheon, Dick Scheumann, Harry MacDonald and Earl Palmer. Mike introduced me to Young Life when I was in high school. Dick discipled me in the faith when I was a young Christian. Harry and Earl were mentors during my college days and helped provide a solid base of theology.

—To a dear friend, Homer Hensley, hindered by cerebral palsy, for helping me understand what it means to be content in all circumstances. He has been an inspiration to many.

—To a wonderful group of close friends who have walked my journey with me over many years: Jack and Jill Miller, Conrad and Judi Jacobsen, Evan and Gloria Otteson, Marcia

i

Otteson, John and Lois Heetderks, Doug and Debbie Burleigh. Everyone should have friends like these.

—To a whole list of Young Life staff, present and former, board members, committee members, club leaders, all too numerous to name. They have befriended me in many ways over the last 35 years.

—To the Board of Directors of our non-profit organization, *Family Insights,* who have been very encouraging and supportive of this entire project. They've all been terrific.

—To a dear friend, Ann Thornfeldt, who lost her long struggle with cancer last year; for her inspiring example of faith and courage.

—To my long time friend, Bill Marshall, for his spiritual insights and humor, which have encouraged a lasting friendship.

—To my friend Uli Chi, a very gifted individual, who saw the potential in this venture and became a special encourager.

—To another good friend, Bob Farrell, who, by his life, showed me the importance of taking a risk. He taught me to be determined in your cause if it is right and will benefit others.

—To several other friends who have encouraged the *Family Insights* seminars, and this book, by their faithful support.

—To all those who have participated in the seminars over the years. It's been a pleasure to work with you.

—To Dr. Gregory Jantz, founder and director of *The Center for Counseling and Health Resources, Inc.* His encouragement and suggestions have been invaluable.

—To Elaine Wright Colvin, director of *Writers' Information Network,* for her tenacity in teaching me how to put together a quality manuscript.

—To Ann McMurray, for her creative ideas, editing and polishing the entire manuscript.

—To Chuck and Athena Dean of *WinePress Publishing,* for their optimistic approach in helping me bring this book project to completion.

—To many other friends who have crossed my path over the years. They have enriched my life by their presence and warmth of friendship. To each, I say a heart-felt "Thank you."

Terry Olsen
Redmond, Washington

INTRODUCTION

"The hard truth is that something has gone wrong with America. There are obvious signs pointing to the moral, spiritual and cultural decline of our nation. These are not good things to get used to." So stated William Bennett, former Secretary of Education, in a speech given to the Heritage Foundation in Washington, D.C.[1]

I submit to you that the moral and spiritual fiber of our nation is breaking down. Much of the decline in our country, I believe, is linked to the decline in the nurturing of America's children by their fathers.

This is a book written with the determined intent of helping bring forth new generations of fathers who understand the significance of being there for their children. Many parents have done an outstanding job preparing children for adult life and responsible citizenship. Somehow, though, over the past few decades we have lost, misplaced, forgotten or forfeited the high calling of fatherhood.

Children have suffered through their growing years from a lack of Dad in the home. Recently, one angry young man told me his parents robbed him of his childhood. Entering adult life full of hostility, he has little regard for a father who is successful in business, but a failure as a father. This bitter young man tells of a childhood where his father was seldom present and when he was, his speech was full of criticism, cynicism and negativism.

So many negative, destructive trends in our society, I believe, can be traced back to a lack of a nurturing father in the home. Statistics show nearly 40% of America's children will go to sleep tonight without their biological fathers tucking them in. More than half of all children will spend at least part of their childhood in a fatherless home.[2]

Apart from positive role models and fatherly guidance, the children of this nation seem to unravel before our very eyes. "Boys, in particular, need male role models. Without a father, who will help them define what it means to be a man? Fathers do things for their children that mothers often don't. It is men who teach boys how to be fathers."[3] And how to treat women.

Girls need fathers in their lives, too. Their father is the first man she will ever love, the first man who will ever love her. So much of her future happiness in relationships depend on her initial relationship with her father.

My Father, My Hero: Becoming Your Child's Best Friend is not meant to be an exhaustive in-depth study of fatherhood. Many of you will be able to add your own suggestions to what is written in this book. It is simply put forward as a means to instruct and encourage fathers in the wonderful, and taxing, process of nurturing your children.

There are inspiring stories, practical experiences and helpful hints to encourage all fathers, fathers-to-be, step-fathers and grandfathers. Hopefully, all fathers will be helped as, together, we seek to reverse our nation's decline and provide the next generation with a message of hope. They deserve a bright future, free from the fears we struggle with today.

Reversing a trend is not always easy. A decision must be made. Men, it's time to make that decision to incorporate significant changes. There is a time for everything under heaven, says the book of Ecclesiastes. A time to be born and a time to die.[4] Perhaps now is the time for old patterns toward fathering to die and new patterns to be born to life. Choosing to be a good dad may mean choosing some new patterns in your fathering style.

There are three kinds of people, the saying goes, "Those who make things happen. Those who watch things happen. And those who say, 'What happened?'"

At the end of your life, as the curtain drops on your performance, will your children stand up and cheer? How will they remember you as a father?

My hope is this book will provide a source of practical encouragement to make things happen with your children.

My prayer is for your children to be able to say, "My father was the best dad anyone could have! He was my hero and my best friend!"

MY CHILDREN'S DAD

*I may never be as clever as my neighbor down the
    street.
I may never be as wealthy as some others that I
    meet.
I may never have the fortune or fame that some
    men have.
But my goal's to be successful...as my children's
    dad.*

*There are certain dreams I cherish, I'd like them to
    come true.
Accomplishments to do before my working days
    are through.
But the task my heart is set on—not just a passing
    fad—
I've just got to be successful...as my children's dad!*

*That's the job I dream of, the task I think of most.
If I fail with my children, I've nothing else to
    boast.
For wealth and fame I'd gather, but my fortune
    would be sad,
If I failed to be successful...as my children's dad.*

*I may never come to glory. I may never gather
    gold.
And men may count a failure when my business
    life is told.
When my children grow up godly, then, I will be
    glad.
For I'll know I've been successful...as my
    children's dad.*

AUTHOR UNKNOWN

Chapter One......DAD THE HERO

The Importance of Dad in the Life of a Child

Charles Francis Adams was a very busy man. A successful lawyer, a member of the House of Representatives and an ambassador to Great Britain, his responsibilities left him little time to spare. Being an organized and meticulous man, he kept a diary of his activities.

"Went fishing with my son today," one entry read. "A wasted day!" it concluded. No grand details of political schemes. No recitations of the important events revolving around his life as a lawyer, representative or ambassador. Only a day off with his son. As far as he was concerned, a totally wasted day.

As it happened, Charles Adam's son, Brooks, also kept a diary. He must have emulated his father early on, for he started keeping a diary while still quite young. On the same date his father had written off as "wasted," young Brooks also made an entry.

"Went fishing with my father today!" he wrote. The words almost shouted the breathless excitement he felt. Instead of considering the day wasted, Brooks had another interpretation. "It was," he said, "the most wonderful day of my life!"[1]

1

* * * * *

Just how important is a father in the life of a child? Do dads really make a difference? If we could look through the eyes of a child, the insignificant moments of our lives would take on new meaning.

When my son, John, was four years old, I was heavily involved as a leader in *Young Life*. As an organization for Christian outreach to high school students, it meant several meetings weekly. I was also away from home a good deal of the time: speaking at camps, playing pick-up basketball games, attempting to build bridges of friendship with as many young people as I could. Looking back on all this activity, I have humorously said, "I was getting myself confused with the Second Person of the Trinity!" While I was very good at building those relationships through my work, I was failing with my relationships at home. It wasn't long before my wife warned me John needed more of my attention. I stopped long enough to listen to what she had to say.

Doing something was harder than just listening. It meant I had to write in time for my son into my already-crowded schedule. Thursday afternoon at 1:30 in the afternoon became "John's time." I would arrive home and John would inform me what he wanted to do.

Often it meant going to the Seattle-Tacoma airport and riding the subway trains in and around the terminal. We'd ride to the north satelite, then back to the main terminal. Then we'd transfer to the south satelite car and ride it to the main terminal. Back and forth. Back and forth.

John would ride up in front, pretending he was the engineer. With everything computerized, there was no real engineer to thwart his imagination. John thought this was great fun. I would endure.

Not every Thursday was spent at the airport, of course. Other days, John would decide we should throw the ball, go kite flying or play with trucks.

One day, my mother wanted to take John on a trip to see my younger brother. He lived in a small community several hours drive from Seattle. As they were discussing when they could go, my mother suggested Thursday.

"Grandma," my son replied, "I can't go on Thursday. That's the day I give to Dad."

The time we spend with our children is important to them.

The Bonding Process

Do you have a story of your own? When was the last quantity time you spent with a son or daughter? We must be aware of the bonding process and its significance in the development of a child's self-worth. Locked tightly within our work routines and outside activities, we allow those days of early childhood to fly by. Before we know it, we're asking ourselves, "Where has the time gone?"

If we are not careful, the opportunities to build a lasting closeness with our children will slip away. There is a time for building relationships with our children. A time for creating the chemistry of togetherness--that time is during childhood.

Where Did The Time Go?

Listen to one father's lament:

"I wish I could have spent more time with my kids, but I was too busy working. After all, I wanted to give them all the things I never had when I was growing up.

"I loved the idea of coming home when they were small and having them sit on my lap to tell me all about their day. Unfortunately, most days I came home so late I was only able to kiss them goodnight after they'd already gone to bed.

"It's amazing how fast kids grow. Before I knew it, they were in junior high. The school productions where they so proudly played clouds and pieces of fruit were gone. I'd missed them. I always seemed to be tied up with something at work or off traveling to a convention. Everyone said they were terrific. The kids never complained, but I could see it in their eyes.

"I kept promising I'd have more time 'next year.' The higher up the corporate ladder I climbed, the less time I seemed to have for the kids.

"Before I knew it, they were teenagers! I wasn't there to see my daughter dressed up for her first prom night. I missed the championship game for my son's basketball team. I tried to call them before they left the house but I could tell by their voices it wasn't enough.

"My kids are in college now. My job is less demanding and I finally have time for them. But my son is out of state and my daughter has her own interests. She doesn't have time for me. To be honest, it hurts not spending more time with them.

"I'd give anything to live those years over. You can bet your life, I'd do it differently. They're out of the house now, and it seems like it's too late."[2]

* * * * *

For several years as a single parent, my children lived with me. I was forced by our circumstances to spend time with them. Since there was no one else, I tried to become involved in their activities. I even became a "Room Mother" for my daughter's class at school and joined the Camp Fire Girls carpool. As a single parent, I had no other parent to shield me from the multitude of needs that children have. I was it. I began to see things from a different perspective.

Many times I would pray, "Lord, help me to see things from their point of view." When out shopping with Megen, I learned it was okay to look...and look some more....and look even more. I learned it was smart to compare prices....and finally go back to the first store and buy the original item. I learned not to say, "Hurry up, Megen!" or "Choose one and let's go!" Shopping through her eyes, I learned to block off more time.

Regularly, however, it occurred to me the Lord was teaching patience.

More Time With Dad

As part of the research for this book, I asked students and adults questions about their own fathers. One of the questions I asked was, "If you could tell your own father one thing, what would it be?

The overwhelming response, though not surprising, was, "I would say to him, 'Dad, I wish we could have spent more time together.'"

I don't suppose there is a father anywhere who could honestly say, "I think I'm spending too much time with my kids!"

Children today are in desperate need of more time with Dad. If we took more time to listen to what they are telling us, we would re-program our priorities. We'd spend less time in board rooms and more time with skateboards. We'd spend less time with co-workers and more time with family. We'd spend less time at work and more time at play...with our kids.

You're A Hero

With great patience, far beyond her five short years, she waited at the window. Every fifteen minutes though her patience would wear thin and she'd run to the kitchen to ask her mother, "When's Daddy coming home?"

"Soon, hon," her mother replied. "You should be able to see his lights coming down the street any time now. Just go look and wait."

So she waited....and waited. She couldn't stand it until he got home. There was so much she wanted to tell him. She also had a very important question to ask.

She was just about to hop off of the couch and run into the kitchen again when she saw the tell-tale double circles of light pulling slowly up against the curb in front of the house.

"Daddy's home!" she yelled at the top of her lungs to no one in particular. Catapulting off the sofa, she ran to the door and threw it open. Her father barely had time to adjust his briefcase before she barrelled into his arms.

"Hi honey," he said, giving her a big hug. "Did you miss me?"

"Of course, Daddy! I always miss you when you go to work!" she replied, looking up at him as if he'd asked the most stupid question in the world.

"What did you do at kindergarden today?" he asked as they went inside the house.

"Daddy! Mrs. Fowler told me today that Wednesday is my "sharing day."

"That's tomorrow. What exactly is a "sharing day?" he asked, putting down his daughter on the floor and his briefcase on the counter.

"It's where you bring something to class you're *very* proud of, like a rock or a picture you made. But I want to bring something else!"

"What's that, honey?" he asked, looking down at his daughter. "What are you *very* proud of?"

"You, Daddy," she said matter-of-factly. "I'm most proud of you."

* * * * *

There's a proverb that says, "The glory of children is in their fathers." (Proverbs 17:6 BV). What does that word "glory" mean? It means to boast about, to take pride in, to praise, even to rejoice about. Wow!

Dad, you're a hero to your children. They love and believe in you! You're bigger than life to a small child.

You're dad. They eagerly await your arrival home each day. Even though you will disappoint them and make mistakes, they will believe in you. Such is the nature of a hero. Such is the responsibility of a hero.

But with the responsibility comes a great significance. The meaning of your life in the heart of a child can never be underestimated. Throughout my years of counseling, one thing has become very clear to me as I've worked with children and adults facing problems in their lives. Much of the time, their inability to cope with life and its problems stem from a poor relationship with their fathers. Without a hero in their life, molehills seem like mountains.

God's Care and Concern

I can still remember the expectation I felt waiting for the birth of my children. Of course, there was the excitement and rush to the hospital. I remember the pride I felt hurrying to the phone to call my family and friends. "Mom and baby are fine! We had a boy!" with John. "We have a beautiful baby girl!" when Megen was born.

It all seemed so miraculous. In just nine months, a living, breathing, squalling baby; a precious gift from God. Being a father allowed me to share a piece of God's creative ability.

God does not take our role as father lightly. The Psalmist says, "Sons are a heritage from the Lord, children a reward from him." (Psalm 127:3 NIV) Children are given to us by God, as is our role of father. He is most interested in how we accomplish this task. After all, they were His before they are ours. Psalm 139 says, "For you created my inmost being; you knit me together in my mother's womb. I praise you because I am fearfully and wonderfully made; your works are wonderful. I know that full well."[3]

7

God has never considered little children to be of little importance. He is intimately concerned with their development from the time of conception through their years of life. During those years, He has given us, as fathers, the role of teaching our children well. He has also given us the privilege of learning from our children.

In the book of Matthew, Jesus reminded us how much we can learn from children. When his disciples were concerning themselves with position and power (as so many of us fathers concern ourselves with today) Jesus called a little child to come and stand next to him.

"I tell you the truth," He told them. "Unless you change and become like little children, you will never enter the kingdom of heaven."[4]

God places great value in children and so should we. We are told to become like children with our heavenly Father and we are warned against treating children badly.

"If anyone causes one of these little ones to stumble," Jesus goes on to say, "it would be better for him to have a large millstone hung around his neck and to be drowned in the depths of the sea."[5]

All of these passages remind us that our Creator sees His creation, our children, as very important people.

Job One

As men in today's society, you wear many hats. You are workers, community leaders, church members, family members. But of all the jobs you have, your role as father should take a high priority in life.

Your children need you more than ever, dad! They need your caring when they're hurt. They need your guidance when they're confused. They need your discipline when they're unruly. They need your time...always.

From you they take their cues about how to respond to life. From you they gain a sense of direction. From you they obtain the security to live a stable life. From you springs their sense of self-worth, their pride in themselves, and even their understanding of "a job well done."

God says children are important, and so are you. To you is given the task of safeguarding all the special qualities of children: their innocence and trust, their full-steam-ahead zest for life, their endless desire for play and laughter, their wonderful acceptance of themselves and others.

One of the best ways I know to accomplish that task comes from the lines of a song:

"Did you ever know that you're my hero?
And everything that I'd like to be?
I can fly higher than an eagle,
For you are the wind beneath my wings."
(Wind Beneath My Wings)[6]

THE BOTTOM LINE

Children long for their father's presence and approval. You're their hero, Dad!

1. In a sentence or two, how would you describe your father?

2. In what ways do you feel you bonded with your father?

3. Can you recall a time when your father was really proud of you?

4. Describe a time when you felt really close with your father.

5. What would your children say about you?

Chapter Two......DAD THE COMPANION

My Dad was always there for me.

Waves of energy ripped across the ground in Armenia that day in 1989. An earthquake of 8.2 magnitude nearly flattened the country. In less than four minutes, thirty thousand people were dead.

In the midst of the initial chaos and utter devastation, a father left his wife safe at home and set off to look for his son. At that time of day, his son would be at school. With panic clutching his throat, he ran towards the school. The closer he got to the building, the more he realized the worst had happened. The school, with his son inside, was toppled to the ground, flat as a pancake.

Tears began to fill his eyes as he looked at the terrible pile of rubble. It looked so hopeless, but he remembered a promise he'd made to his son; "No matter what, I'll always be there for you."

Terror threatened to take away all reason, but he struggled to concentrate on where his son might be in the building. He remembered where he always walked his son to class each morning. Starting in the back right corner of the building, he began to methodically dig through the debris.

So focused was he on his work that he barely noticed when other frightened parents arrived. Each, in turn, would clutch their heart or raise their hands to the sky and scream the name of their child.

"It's too late!" one man said, trying to pull him away from his task. "They're dead. There's nothing you can do."

Others told him, "You can't help. You're only making it worse."

The father listened to each, then said, "Are you going to help me now?" Stone by stone, he continued to dig for his son.

The fire chief of the town finally arrived and tried to pull him away from the debris. "Fires are breaking out," he told the father gently. "Explosions are happening everywhere. You're in danger here. You must go home and let us take care of things here."

"Are you going to help me now?"

The fire chief left him to dig.

Before long, a police officer came. "Please," he told the father. "You're distraught. You're endangering yourself and others. You must go home!"

To which the father asked, "Are you going to help me now?"

No one came to help him. No one believed there was anyone left, not even the father was sure. He had to know, though, if his son was dead or alive. He dug for eight hours which turned into twelve hours. Twelve hours turned into twenty-four. Whenever his tired body was tempted to stop, he thought of his son, alive under all that rubble. Twenty-four hours drug on into thirty-six.

During the thirty-eighth hour of digging for his son, the father heaved a boulder off the pile. Softly he heard a voice rising up through the debris.

"Dad?" the voice asked, weakly.

"Armand!" screamed the father, new energy fueling a frantic desire to rip through the pile.

"Dad! It's me, Dad! I told the other kids not to worry. I told them that if you were still alive, you'd come for me. And when you came for me, you'd save them, too."

"How many of you are there?" his father asked, throwing bricks and lifting chunks of concrete.

"Fourteen of us are left, Dad. When the school collapsed, the roof made a wedge, like a triangle. It saved us. We're hungry and thirsty and scared," the boy told his father. "I'm so glad you came for me!"

By this time, his father had widened a hole big enough for his son to crawl out. "Armand," he told him, "Come on out!" He could barely wait until his eyes could see his son, alive.

"Not yet, Dad," Armand replied through the darkness. "Let the other kids go out first. I know, no matter what, you'll be there for me!"[1]

*　*　*　*　*

I am so inspired by that story. I can't imagine what it would be like to almost lose a child that way. I like to think that I could be that father, digging relentlessly until his child was safe. All of us would like to be that father; to have that kind of devotion and strength. Unfortunately, many fathers don't. In my counseling practice, I hear about those fathers that fail all the time. Sometimes I hear when I least expect.

While working on this book, I went to an office supply store. The clerk was friendly and asked if I'd found everything I needed.

"Yes," I told her. "I just came for these disks. I need a few more to finish a book I'm writing."

"You're writing a book?" she asked, interested. "What about?"

"It's about fathers and how important they are in a child's life," I responded. "I'm trying to encourage dads to be nurturers of their children, to build self-esteem and security in their kids."

"That sounds nice," she said, wistfully. "Too late for me, though. My father died last year."

"I'm sorry to hear that. At least you were able to be with him for this long," I told her, thinking of the children I'd known whose fathers had died when they were very young.

"Not really," she said, rather sorrowfully. "Even when he was alive, he was never there for me."

Talking with her made me remember that simply *existing* around our children isn't enough. We need to *establish a presence* in the life of our children.

A Father's Presence

Those who know and understand parenting tell us there are at least four factors children need to help them build healthy emotional lives. Your presence, Dad, will help provide your children with these four needed ingredients:

Recognition - All children need to know they count. Each one needs to realize how valuable they are. Fathers enable their children to feel valuable by giving recognition to them as individuals. Along with recognition, they also need approval.

Response - Children need somthing they can give themselves to. They need something worthwhile they can be a part of- -a cause to be excited about, to respond to. Camp Fire Girls, Cub Scouts, Indian Guides, Awana, Little League are all organizations that allow children to move beyond themselves and their small world. In this way, they gain recognition and worth from being a member of a team.

Adventure - Here is an area where dads can excel! There are so many things we can do to bring a sense of adventure into our children's lives. Often, this area is overlooked. Children can create their own world of adventure and excitement without too much help, of course. Watching a group of pre-schoolers track down the bad-guy or sail a pirate ship made out of a refrigerator box shows you their adventurous spirit. While they can play on their own, there are few things they enjoy more than adventure play with Dad! The adventures are much more thrilling when Dad is along for the ride!

Security - Security can mean several things. It can refer to a home to live in for shelter. Security can be basic necessities, such as food or clothing. But it goes beyond the realm of mere physical requirements. Security is also the emotional feeling that all is well within the family. Children need to know that all is okay with Mom and Dad, especially Dad.

There is great security in feeling loved and in being appreciated. Feeling valued and cared for are steady anchors in a stormy crisis. Most of all, security is found in knowing that Dad (or Mom) are always there for them, whether they've scraped a knee or bruised an ego.

The Prodigal's Father

One of the most wonderful stories in the Bible is found in the book of Luke. Most of the time it is told with an emphasis on the wayward or prodigal son, but I like to think of it as a parable about a steadfast dad.

The story goes that the younger son of a father became discontent with his life at home. He decided, therefore, to obtain his share of the inheritance from his father early. With the money in hand, off he went to a distant country. Once there, he squandered his inheritance completely on bad companions and poor choices.

His desperate plight became even harder when a famine came over the land. Since the young man had no money, he hired himself out to a local citizen. He was given charge over a herd of pigs. Finding himself continually hungry, he even began to envy the slop of his charges.

One day while mucking around with the pigs, he suddenly had a revelation. "Even my father's workers have food left over and here I am, starving to death! I'll go back home to my father and say to him, 'Father, I've sinned against heaven and against you. I'm not worthy to be called your son. I'll be happy if you'll make me just one of your hired hands.'"

So the young man went home. While he was still a far way off, his father saw him. The sight of his son coming home filled him with compassion. He called for a feast to be prepared and clothes brought for his son. So glad was he to have him home, a celebration began. *(Luke 15:11-32 NIV)*

A Father's Significance

Whichever way I've heard that story emphasized, I've never heard it said the son thought about coming home to *Mom*. Mothers are often known for their great compassion for children who make mistakes, especially big-time mistakes. Many children go back home to mom, hoping she'll be able to smooth things over with dad.

No, this story doesn't say he went home to mom, or to a close friend, or even to his older brother. When the young man thought of going home, he thought of going home to dad.

During our lives, our kids will do many things that will leave us, as parents, disappointed. Their actions leave us hurt, frustrated, and even angry. Sometimes these mistakes will be accidental, sometimes deliberate. When they happen, we need to remember not the story of the prodigal son, but the story of the steadfast, compassionate father.

We need to build up a relationship with our children so that, whatever happens, they know they can always come home to us. They need to know we'll always be there.

16

Teaching Through Trust

When recognition, response, adventure and security blend together in a relationship, trust is built. Once a trusting relationship is established, the ground-work has been laid for teaching your children. They accept your teaching and have confidence they can learn from you. Learning from you at this stage is not the question. The question is what you will teach them.

1. *Teach your children about God.* You can do this both through words and through actions. Let your child see that your religion is a relationship. Help them to understand your relationship with God and guide them into their own relationship with Jesus Christ.

In a broader sense, few things will be as important to your child's relationship with their Heavenly Father as their relationship with you. The pattern they develop for being a child of God is influenced by being your child. What children learn about fathers comes first from you.

2. *Teach your children about the world around them.* Talk about the things in nature. Help them understand how this world works together: the animals and plants, the sunshine and the rain, the moon and the stars. By giving this world a sense of order, your child gains confidence. Fear usually is heightened by the unknown. Dangers explained are dangers more easily faced.

3. *Teach your children to play games.* This is not all fun and games. Sure, fun is part of it. In addition, though, games teach children valuable lessons. Children learn the value of unity and togetherness during team play. This helps them understand the importance of working with others and getting along.

Teachable moments with your kids come when you least expect them. It may be while driving in the car, walking down the street, sitting at the dinner table, snuggling together right before bed. Our lives are so busy, kids lives are, too. When teaching times come, take advantage of them. Nurture these times by maintaining a relationship of trust with your children.

Children Learn What They Live

Raising emotionally healthy children takes a concerted effort. It is not only what we teach them verbally, but also the messages we pass on to them through our actions. One of the best things I've ever read about this, comes from a familiar poem by an anonymous author.

If a child lives with criticism, He learns to condemn.
If a child lives with hostility, He learns to fight.
If a child lives with ridicule, He learns to be shy.
If a child lives with shame, He learns to feel guilty.
If a child lives with tolerance, He learns to be patient.
If a child lives with encouragement, He learns confidence.
If a child lives with praise, He learns to appreciate.
If a child lives with approval, He learns to like himself.
If a child lives with acceptance and friendship,
He learns to find love in the world.[2]

We can tell children all we want, but they will filter our words through our actions. As fathers we must not only teach the lessons of life, we must model them as well.

To Be There or Not To Be There

Let's face it- - most of us dads are not very good nurturers by nature. We can put together a bike on Christmas Eve in the dark, but we're out of our league mending a broken heart. Many of the challenges of every day life leave us feeling insecure and unprepared. In order to avoid this feeling of helplessness, we tend to remain uninvolved with those everyday-life kind of activities. It is easier to withdraw both physically and emotionally.

"That's why mothers were invented," we tell ourselves. "She is so much more capable of handling this situation. I'll just let her deal with it." This trend toward none or little involvement needs to be reversed.

If you are a dad who is out of the home, nearly all of the daily happenings of family life will escape you. Whether you are away at work a good deal of the time, or a divorce has removed you from a daily interaction with your children, I urge you to stay connected. As much as possible, touch base with each of your children daily.

I have many friends who have gone through a painful separation or divorce. Still they have managed to be a father to their children. This hasn't been easy. It has meant juggling schedules, dealing with their kid's mother and relatives, and working hard to keep the lines of communication open with their kids. But if you ask their children, they will tell you, "My Dad is always there for me."

A Father Who Was There

The weekend arrived. It was time to get caught up on all the chores that somehow never made it to completion during the week. Mom headed out to the grocery store trailing a list of errands half a mile long. Dad decided it would be a good time to work on the leaky faucet in the kitchen. Brother and Sister were out in the backyard, playing and watching their younger brother, Kenny. Kenny's job, at seven, was not to get into too much trouble. He decided to play near the family dock beside the lakefront.

Brother and Sister soon got distracted, and when Dad came out to check on things, wiping pipe grease off of his hands, Kenny was nowhere in sight.

"Where's Kenny?" Dad asked, allowing a touch of anxiety to enter his voice.

"He was right there playing a second ago," answered Brother, pointing toward the dock.

Dad walked over to the dock. Sure enough, there was a half-eaten peanut butter and jelly sandwich melting in the sun. He swept his eyes over the surface of the water Kenny's new baseball cap floated near the dock.

Immediately, Dad jumped into the water and began to search the area at the end of the dock. The water was deep there and the light barely worked its way in. Swimming around stirred up silt from the bottom. The clouds of dirt obscured his view even more. Running out of air, he surfaced.

Taking another big gulp, he dove back down under the water. Circling wildly with his arms, he searched for any sign of his son. He kicked over toward the dock pilings. Working his way around the slimy supports, he felt something. Then that something moved. It was Kenny! Prying him quickly from the piling, they surfaced together. Both gasped deeply for air. Brother and Sister helped Dad lift Kenny up onto the dock. Dad followed, dragging himself out of the water. Together they lay exhausted, stretched out on the warm wood.

"Kenny, what happened?" Dad asked when he could finally speak. "How'd you fall in?"

"I don't know, Dad," Kenny replied, like any kid trying to explain a difficult situation. "I just don't know."

"Well, what were you doing down there?" Dad asked, allowing his exasperation to surface. "What were you hanging onto the dock for?!"

"Waiting for you, Dad," Kenny replied, matter-of-factly. "Just waiting for you."[3]

20

THE BOTTOM LINE

*Children don't care what you know,
until they know that you care.*

1. Can you recall an event in your life when
    you really needed your father to be there
    for you? Was he? What feelings did you
    have?

2. What are the times when you have "been
    there" for your own children? How did
    "being there" make you feel?

3. Looking back, do you feel like there were
    times you should have "been there" for
    a son or daughter, but weren't?

4. What are the most important things you
    feel you are teaching your children?

Chapter Three......DAD THE EXAMPLE

Do as I say, not as I do.

"Michael!" his father warned sternly, "you shouldn't have brought those school pencils home!" Michael hung his head and didn't say anything.

"Don't you know," his father continued, "I can get you *plenty* of pencils from the office!"

* * * * *

"They'll never know, Dad!" Billy whispered. "I can easily pass for eleven! Besides, it's a buck fifty!"

For a moment, Billy's father was tempted. After all, it was just a movie--the price break for kids, twelve and under. His son turned twelve two months before. What would it hurt? And like Billy said, it was a buck fifty!

Together, Billy and his father walked up to the ticket window. "I'd like some tickets, please," he said, Billy tugging furtively at the hem of his jacket. "Two *adults*, please."

Billy had a quizzical look on his face, as his father waited for the change. "They'd never know the difference, Dad," he complained, as they walked inside.

"That's true, son," his father said, handing him his ticket. "But I would know, and so would you."

*   *   *   *   *

Two different ways of dealing with everyday situations. No grand test of integrity with your back to the wall, choosing between virtuous right and despicable evil. Just commonplace incidents, the kind that happen all of the time.

While the details might slip your mind easily, the lessons learned by your children are indelible. They will remember. Children constantly look for direction and guidance on how to navigate the unchartered waters of growing up. They watch and learn and are very adept at detecting which way the wind is blowing. During their early, formative years, what you do is important. Your words, actions, and reactions are being transferred into impressionable minds.

Fathering is Role Modeling

"He's a chip off the old block!"
"The tiny acorn doesn't fall far from the mighty oak."
"Like father, like son."

Whether we like it or not, our children pick up our characteristics. Roles, as men and fathers, are passed along. Too many men never stop to ask themselves the question, "Am I being a good role model to my children?"

Most of us do better at household roles of plumber, carpenter or auto mechanic. We like being "Mr. Fix-it" with problems we can tackle quickly and move on. Unlike an occasional leaky faucet, squeaky door hinge or punctured tire, the process of role modeling goes on every minute. There isn't a "quick fix." Being a father involves each minute, each hour. Then, just when you get a handle on it, the kids leave the house.

If you are fortunate, in due time, grandchildren will appear. Like it or not, you will be a role model for someone your entire life. It's time to start thinking about the kinds of characteristics you are modeling.

24

Modeling Integrity

"Oh, what a tangled web we weave when first we practice to deceive."[1]

This famous quote, by Sir Walter Scott, shows the flipside of honesty and integrity. One small step of dishonesty leads to another small step, becoming a giant leap. Eventually, the conscience is seared. Truth becomes a stranger from which you hide as wrongful deeds are denied to self and others. You end up living a lie.

Honesty, on the other hand, frees you from the weight of a guilty conscience. Relationships are easier to develop and maintain when you have a good reputation.

If there is one characteristic a father should teach his children, it's honesty. Honesty can be hard and children learn early how to "manipulate" the facts to gain an advantage.

"I didn't see who knocked over the lamp!" *I know Timmy did it, but I wasn't actually in the room when it happened.*

"I didn't know it was my bedtime!" *I purposely kept from looking at the clock so I wouldn't know what time it was.*

"Brother hit me!" *Of course, I hit him first, but I won't mention that.*

Kids figure out how to lie, conceal, and misdirect on their own. Sadly, in our society today, taking advantage of someone else or lying isn't always discouraged. The only negative consequence is getting caught. Damage to self or others is rarely emphasized.

If society will not emphasize the inner values and qualities, then , as fathers, we must. We must take every opportunity, no matter how insignificant it might seem, to teach our children to be people of honesty and integrity.

The apostle, Paul, in his defense before Felix, the governor, said, "I strive always to keep my conscience clear before God and man." (Acts 24:16 NIV) May each of us strive to say that statement and enable our children to do the same.

Follow The Leader

As father and son opened the door, they were greeted by a blast of cold air. Mornings in February could be especially brisk, with new fallen snow blanketing the ground. They bundled scarves and hats tighter.

"Ready to go?" the father asked, his voice muffled through the scarf.

"Sure, Dad," his son replied. "How far do we have to go this morning?"

They carefully manuvered down the icy steps toward the barn, about fifty yards off.

"We need to check and see if the storm knocked over any trees near the pasture fence. Shouldn't take too long. We'll be inside and warm again before you know it."

The way was slow going because of the fresh coat of snow. As they moved out away from the buildings, the snow became deeper.

"How'ya doin', son?" the father asked, looking over to his right. His son was furiously working short legs back and forth through the thigh-deep snow. "It's just a little farther," he called encouragingly.

They continued on in silence, heads bowed to the wind, their breath sending out clouds of frost into the air. "We'll stop and rest up here, son," the father said without looking up.

It startled him when he heard, "Okay," coming not from beside him but behind him.

"Whatcha doin' back there?" he asked, stopping.

"I decided to follow you, Dad. It's a lot easier walking where you've already been!" Sure enough, his son was jumping happily from footprint to footprint.

*　*　*　*　*　*

26

Throughout our lives , we leave footprints. Others will follow because we have marked the way. We are trailblazers for our children. As fathers, we need to be very careful to mark the right path for our children. Where we lead, they follow.

A common path provided for children is outlined in the words of a well-known song called, *"Cats In The Cradle"* by Harry Chapin. It goes:

My child arrived just the other day,
    He came in the world in the usual way.
    But there were planes to catch and bills to pay.
    He learned to walk while I was away.
And He was talkin' 'fore I knew it, and as he grew,
    He said, "I'm gonna be like you, Dad.
    "You know, I'm gonna be like you."

My son turned ten just the other day.
    He said, "Thanks for the ball, Dad. Come on, let's play.
    "Can you teach me to throw?"
    I said, "Not today. I got a lot to do."
    He said, "That's okay."
And he walked away, but his smile never dimmed.
    It said, "I'm gonna be like him, yeah.
    "You know, I'm gonna be like him."

And the cat's in the cradle and the silver spoon.
    Little boy blue and the man-on-the-moon.
    "When you comin' home?"
    "Son, I don't know when. But we'll get together then.
    "You know, we'll have a good time then."

Well, he came from college just the other day.
 So much like a man, I just had to say,
 "Son, I'm proud of you. Can you sit for a
while?"
 He shook his head and said with a smile,
"What I'd really like, Dad, is to borrow the car
keys.
 "See ya later. Can I have them, please?"

I've long since retired. My son's moved away.
 I called him up just the other day.
 I said, "I'd like to see you, if you don't mind."
 He said, "I'd love to, Dad, if I can find the
time.
"You see, my new job's a hassle and the kids have
 the flu.
 "But it's been sure nice talkin' to you, Dad.
 "It's sure nice talkin' to you."
And as I hung up the phone, it occurred to me,
 He'd grown up just like me.
 My boy was just like me!

And the cat's in the cradle and the silver spoon.
 Little boy blue and the man-on-the-moon.
 "When you comin' home?"
 "Dad, I don't know when. But we'll get
 together, then, Dad.
 "You know, we'll have a good time, then."[2]

Our children will model our example, for better or worse. Be the kind of person, today, you want your child to become tomorrow.

A Look At Priorities

Being a good role model, for our children, means having our priorities straight. If your children were asked

28

what they thought your priorities were, what would they say? Most kids would respond with something like: "The most important things in my dad's life are: his job, watching sports, or playing sports." Some might even get around to friends, family, and church.

Setting our priorities in order is one of hardest things to do. How many of us have started a New Year's Resolution and wound up admitting defeat by the middle of February? I find having an appropriate number one priority helps everything else fall into place. I admit I haven't always been diligent in maintaining priorities, but when I have, peace and stability followed.

Priority Number One: My number one priority is my relationship to God. I can't be a good father to my children until I'm a good child to my Father. Having an active faith in God has helped me to have peace and direction in my life. When the stress and press of other priorities try to derail my relationship with Jesus Christ, I fight hard to maintain it. I do not believe I could have made it through the daily struggles in this life without it.

Priority Number Two: Next in priority should be family. A religious tie is important, but it should not negate family relationships. The apostle, Paul, in writing to a young friend in the faith called Timothy, tells him, "If anyone does not provide for his relatives, and especially for his immediate family, he has denied the faith and is worse than an unbeliever." (1 Timothy 5:8 NIV). He was telling Timothy how important God considers family ties. Additionally, he expresses the idea that, by taking care of the needs of your family, you are acting out your faith. The well-being of your family, whether physical, emotional, spiritual or social , should be a constant concern for every father.

Priority Number Three: A third priority, personally very helpful, is a small group of friends who meet together in acceptance and camaraderie. "If you need me, I'll be there," is the attitude of these men.

None of us does a very good job going it alone. We weren't meant to do this job of fathering all by ourselves. By encouraging others, we allow others to encourage us.

Not only has my small group of friends offered me encouragement, I have felt accountable to them. Over the years as we have regularly met, I've found I care what they think of me and the kind of a man I am. Their opinion matters, so I am motived to be more than I could be, alone.

So important is this idea of "accountability" in fathering, I've devoted an entire chapter to its discussion. (Chapter Fourteen)

Priority Number Four: The fourth priority is your job, the way you earn your living. Whether anyone else in the family contributes income, your job helps provide your family's basic needs. This is the responsibility of husband and father.

Your work also provides you with purpose and fulfillment. Be careful, though! Climbing the corporate ladder can be addicting. The praise and monetary reward you receive for a job well done can seem seductively more important than trivial family concerns. An important question to keep asking yourself is, "Why am I working here?" Is the time and energy you are putting into your job a quest for personal glory or a way to fill your financial needs?

Jesus said in Matthew 16:26 (NIV), "What good will it do for a man if he gains the whole world, yet forfeits his soul?"

A Person of Value

"Try not to become a person of success, rather become a person of value. A successful person takes out of life

more than he puts in. A person of value will give more than he receives." Albert Einstein.

Who would say success in business, at any cost, is of greater value than family? Some might have to admit business success has been of greater value than personal integrity. These are men who operate with a "dog-eat-dog" mentality.

In my counseling, I have seen families left in the wake of "success-oriented" men. These men have little personal integrity and fewer friends. Their families are consistently dysfunctional. Their lives, and the lives they touch, become warped by their sense of value. Usually at some point, they stop long enough to realize their values are worthless. A life of "success" has left them empty.

Modeling A Life of Service

Mother Teresa, of Calcutta, India , is a remarkable person. Tiny in stature and wrinkled in appearance, she radiates a powerful presence. It has been said, "People stand in line to see presidents. Presidents stand in line to see Mother Teresa." This little woman has an enormous heart for serving others. In her role as a servant, she leads many.

One of the most difficult concepts to get across to children today is service to others. Too often, the message they hear is, "What's in it for me?"

This world has, once again, gotten it backwards. Conventional logic says, "It is better to receive than give. It is better to be served than to serve." Exceptional wisdom counters, "It is better to give than to receive. It is better to serve than to be served." This is, remarkably, something young children know. It's the toddler fetching dad his tools during a difficult repair. It's the five-year old who gently carries a dandelion puff home as a gift. It's the excited child who can't wait, shouting, "Go on, Daddy. Open it!" at a birthday.

Somehow we must preserve that child-like heart and guard it through adolescence.

One vital way is to model a servant's heart to your children and spouse. It may take you considerable effort to overcome the messages of this world, but keep at it! Soon you'll find your child actually doing something you want, before you ask! If you model "pitching in" and helping, your children will understand how important service is to you. They'll admire that quality of a servant.

The Next Generation

When I was growing up, my father would always play catch with me. Back and forth, we'd throw the ball. There was a soothing rhythm to the swing of the arm and the thump of the caught ball. I remember those times with great fondness. It wasn't surprising, really, but I seemed to play a lot of catch with my own son, John.

My father also took my brothers and me to sporting events: college basketball games, baseball under the lights. Over the years, I've taken my own children to many similar events. Waiting in the stands for the game to start, munching peanuts or popcorn, made me remember those times with my father.

I've never taken my children fishing. My dad never took me fishing. He went often with friends, but I wasn't invited. He never took me camping or hiking. I haven't taken my own children, even though I've done alot of both with *Young Life.*

My father was a faithful provider. It was his way of showing love. In his time and culture, that was being a "good dad." Sometimes, it wasn't enough. I've tried to be involved with my children in a great deal of activities. I've tried to spend time with each and include them in as many things as I could; from special vacations with friends to quick visits to the mall.

However, as I look back, I find it interesting that those things I did with my dad somehow made it into my kid's schedule. And the things I didn't do with dad, I didn't do with my children. Perhaps when my kids have kids, I'll be able to reverse the trend.

Life Without Father

Forty percent of children in this country go to bed each night without "dad," their biological father, kissing them goodnight or tucking in the covers. So says the *National Fatherhood Initiative*. As I think back on all of the goodnight kisses I've given , on all of the covers I've gently tucked in around sleepy bodies, it makes me very sad.

Statistics say one in three children born in America today are to unwed mothers. No father in the house. No husband in the home. Among the children of divorce, fifty percent have never even visited their father's home. Four out of ten haven't seen their father in a year. Half of those haven't seen him in over five years.

Children, without the presence of a father in their lives, are more likely to experience drug abuse, mental illness, juvenile delinquency, criminal behavior and suicidal tendencies. Sixty-two percent of America's rapists grew up without "Dad" in the home. Seven out of ten teens who kill, and long-term prison inmates, went through childhood without a father present.[3] These are terrible statistics. Even more terrible are the shattered lives which lie behind them. Over and over again, the absence of a father forebodes a difficult time for a child.

Responsible Role Modeling

Fathers, I plead with you to take seriously your responsibility to be a positive role model for your children. All of us must take action if we are to send forth a new generation of young men, who are prepared to be fathers. This won't happen automatically. Fatherhood isn't something best done on auto-pilot.

If we do not take this role seriously, look for our society to continue its downhill slide of moral and spiritual decline. The best way to protect our children from the wrongs which infest this world is to expose them to all that we feel is right.

Lead by example! Choose to be a man of honesty and integrity in all your dealings, from the head of the company to the person behind the ticket counter. Choose to be a servant to your family. Faithfully teach your children about your faith and values.

These are not revolutionary concepts. They were written down by a man thousands of years ago. "These commandments that I give you today are to be upon your hearts. Impress them on your children. Talk about them when you sit at home and when you walk along the road, when you lie down and when you get up." (Deuteronomy 6:6-7 NIV)

"Train up a child in the way he should go, and when he is old he will not turn from it." (Proverbs 22:6 NIV) Our words are so important, but remember, actions speak even louder than words.

There's a poem I like about modeling. It kind of rebuts that age-old excuse, "Do as I say, not as I do."

I'd rather see a sermon, than hear one any day.
I'd rather one should walk with me,
than merely show the way.
The eye's a better pupil, and more willing than the ear.
Fine counsel is confusing, but examples are always clear.
And the best of all the fathers
are the men who live their creeds.
For to see good put into action is what everybody needs.
I can learn to do it, if you'll let me see it done.
I can watch your hand in action,

but your tongue too fast may run.
And the lecture you deliver may be very well and true,
But I'd rather get my lesson by observing what you do.
For I might misunderstand you, the high advice you give.
But there's NO misunderstanding
how you act and how you live.[4]

THE BOTTOM LINE

*Be the kind of person today
you want your child to become
tomorrow.*

1. What positive traits are you passing on, either directly or indirectly to your children?

2. What do you want your children to learn from you?

3. Have you shown your family how to have a "servant's heart?"

4. In the "supermarket" of values, what values would you put into your cart? What would you put back on the shelf?

Chapter Four...DAD THE ENCOURAGER

The Power of Affirmation

"I can live two months on one good compliment." - Mark Twain

I heard about a study that was done in 1991 by a group of researchers. It concerned the conduct of children in the second grade. The researchers observed overall behavior and how the children responded to their teacher.

In one classroom, they found a mad-house. The teacher was constantly asking her young students to remain in their seats.

"Sit down!" she pleaded with them, over and over. Every thirty-three seconds, children in the class would pop up out of their seats.

"Sit down!" she'd say again, every seventy-five seconds.

The researchers asked her to increase her requests, to once every nineteen seconds, to see if shortening the time between each directive would help control the class. It didn't. Her little cherubs continued to get up and wander around the room. The researchers had her go back to her previous pattern..

Next, the teacher was instructed to stop saying, "sit down" to her students. Instead of focusing on those children who constantly got out of their seats, she was requested to pay attention only to the children who remained seated. She was to affirm their good behavior and praise the projects they were working on.

Within twenty minutes, not a single child was out of their seat.

* * * * *

What the teacher in that classroom learned is something all of us as fathers need to remember: Attention + Affirmation + Encouragement = Positive Responses.

The Power of Affirmation

"Thank you."
"Do you know how special you are to me?"
"What a wonderful job you've done!"
"I couldn't have done it without you."
"Honey, it doesn't matter. I still love you."

Affirmation is several things, done in different ways. It is that recognition of another person, that says, "You count." It's encouragement and praise. It's courtesy and kindness which communicates the message, "I value you." Warts and all, affirmation confirms you're still loved.

Unfortunately, affirmation is not a concept readily accepted. We live in a time when put-downs, snide remarks, cheap shots, and sarcasm mark the cultural tone. I recognize, men will engage in good-natured, even cutting, humor with each other as a way of bonding. What I am speaking about are words which wound.

"The tongue is a small part of the body, but it makes great boasts," says the book of James, chapter 3. "Consider what a great forest is set on fire by a small spark. The tongue also is a fire, a world of evil..."

Words cast on the wind are very difficult to reel in, especially the hurtful kind. Too often, our children are the recipients of our inability to control our tongue. How often have we wished we could take something back said in anger? The man who has control of his tongue has control of himself.

"All kinds of animals, birds, reptiles, and creatures of the sea are being tamed and have been tamed by man," James goes on to remind us. "But no man can tame the tongue. It is a restless evil, full of deadly poison. With the tongue we praise our Lord and Father and with it we curse men, who have been made in God's likeness. Out of the mouth come praise and cursing. My brothers, this should not be." (James 3:5-10 NIV)

My brothers, this must not be, for our children's sake.

Building Up or Putting Down

Guard your tongue from hurtful talk,
And words that are unkind.
If you want to know true happiness,
And enjoy peace of mind.[1]

All of us have borne the brunt of hurtful words. Words which, intended or not, wounded us. All of us have experienced a compliment. Which felt better? The affirmation, of course!

In our relationship with our children, it is important to guard the words we use. Praise and encouragement can lift them to new heights of self-worth. Undue criticism can break a spirit. When bonding with our children, we don't want our own personalities to be so domineering, there is no room left for the expression and will of our child.

A child who is constantly criticized begins to lose initiative. To act is to risk rejection. Soon that child will lose excitement about life. Over time, the hurts stuffed inside that little body will produce anger and resentment.

Affirming With *Quantity and Quality* Time

Remember the equation from the teacher at the beginning of this chapter? *Attention + Affirmation + Encouragment = Positive Responses.* Positive responses produce even more affirmation, causing a child to feel good about who they are. This is crucial in developing self-esteem and establishing self-worth.

Self-esteem is built up in a child by the words they hear from mom and dad. Actions, also, speak louder than words. Parents need to be consistent in their messages. It's not enough to say, "Becky, I think you're so special!" if you never spend any time with her. She'll think your other activities are more valuable than she is. It won't matter how many times you say something, she'll be looking at your actions to verify your words.

All of us have heard of the concept of *Quality Time*. It's the idea it's not so important how much time you spend with your children, but what you do with the time you have. If you only have twenty minutes a day with your child, that's enough, if it's intense personal time. For busy, harried parents, this concept seems very appealing. They can say to themselves, "So what if I don't spend much time with my kids? The time I give them is quality time!" But who is to determine if it is quality?

On the other hand is the idea, just being physically present around your children is enough. As long as they can see you, talk to you (whenever you're not busy doing something else) or occupy the same space with you, you've discharged your duty as a parent.

I don't see how you can do an effective job bringing up your children without both quantity and quality time. Every moment you spend with your child isn't going to be meaningful. Every waking hour isn't going to produce those character-building memories. Face it, we're just not that good. No matter how hard we strive to orchestrate a small amount of time with our kids to maximum effect, they simply may not see it that way. But over a quantity of time, as we walk and talk and teach our children, quality time will emerge.

Think back to when you were dating, when you first fell in love. You wanted every moment to be special. You wanted to be with that certain lady every moment! What you felt back then is how your children feel today. You can't build a solid relationship without both quantity and quality time.

Fathers and Quantity Time

How would you describe your father during your childhood years?

____ disciplinarian	____ read to me
____ fun loving	____ gave me hugs
____ workaholic	____ told me he loved me
____ easy going	____ made me feel good
____ took me places	____ helped me with
____ always had time for me	homework
____ perfectionist	____ made me feel bad
____ too strict	____ cared for me when
____ too uptight	I was sick
____ harmony in family	____ was kind to my friends
relationships	____ made Mom feel special
____ too busy	____ made Mom feel bad
____ took me to movies	____ didn't like my friends
____ fun to be with	____ liked our pets
____ took me camping	____ always yelled
____ took me to circus	____ was a good listener
____ came to my ball games	____ other

41

In my research for this book, I surveyed a large number children and adults. I asked them about their fathers, to describe him during their childhood years and list any activities they shared. I've reproduced the survey for you to peruse.

I found an interesting correlation in this survey between time spent on activites and the amount of affirmation given. When dad was described as a workaholic, too busy, or one of the other negative traits, few events or activities were checked. If the quantity of time spent was low, the feelings of affirmation were also low. The opposite was also true. If there was a high amount of activities participated in by father and child, the feelings of worth and affirmation were high.

Giving this survey to your own children could be of great help. Taking the survey yourself about your own father could be very enlightening, too.

Giving Up Some Time

If you care deeply about your child's welfare, give your child all the encouragement and time you can muster. It may mean passing up a golf game with some buddies. It may mean reading the rest of the paper after the kids have gone to bed. It may mean giving up the first half of Monday Night Football. As entertaining as that game might be, the outcome won't make one bit of difference in the friendship between you and your kids. When they're older, invite them to watch the game with you. Being a couch-potato every Monday night, or any other night sports are on, can take a toll on your relationship with all of your family.

Being a father means engaging in sacrifice. Your time, energy, and money are no longer exclusively yours. By having a family, you've entered into a contract to care for that family, to give their needs a priority in your life. Really caring for your kids may mean putting on the back-burner an activity you enjoy. You may have to cut down on the amount of time you spend on it, or stop doing it altogether for a while. Often, when your children are older, you can begin to involve them in activities you enjoy.

A friend of mine was so excited when his daughter was finally old enough to go skiing. She invited a friend along and they drove up to the mountain.

"We can get in some fast runs," he told them, gripping the wheel in anticipation of the wind in his hair, the just-out-of-control plunge down the powdery slope. "I like to take it as 'close to the edge' as I can!"

His headlong rush down the expert run turned into an entire day on the "bunny slope." He was so excited about skiing himself, he forget that his daughter and her friend had seldom skied before. He forgot that ten year olds don't learn something new in a minute.

Down they'd crawl on the bunny slope, the girls falling regularly. He'd pick them up, dust off the snow, and help them on their way.

Near the end of the day, they went into the lodge to warm up with a cup of hot chocolate. The girls were exhausted. They were happy just to sit down by the fire with their chocolate and giggle to themselves about their big day of skiing.

"Honey," he asked his daughter. "Would it be alright if I left you two here for a few minutes, while I go on a run by myself?"

"Sure, Dad," she told him. "We'll stay right here and wait for you."

Hustling to the lift, he headed up the mountain. Stopping briefly at the top, the wind in his hair, he began a just-out-of-control plunge down the powdery slope. It was exhilarating! He headed happily toward the lodge where his two little snow bunnies were still sipping their hot chocolate.

Driving back in the car, he thought about the great day he'd had. It was a grand privilege to spend time with his daughter and her friend in the great outdoors. Though it hadn't turned out exactly as he'd planned, he knew it was a special day for them. And he'd gotten in one run! All in all, it was a very good day. He'd remember the sparkle in their eyes when they skied a yard and didn't fall. His daughter would always remember how her dad made her feel.

Loving Yourself - Loving Others

When my daughter, Megen, was five, we were living in Portland, Oregon. The family was preparing to visit my parents and some friends up north in Seattle, Washington. As we were getting ready to go, Megen kept herself busy and out of the way fingerpainting at the kitchen table.

"What are you making?" I asked, kneeling down beside her chair.

"A picture for Jack," she said, referring to our friend in Seattle.

"Oh, Megen," I told her., "that's so nice of you. Jack will just love your picture." She smiled, making swirls with her goopy hands.

"I love you, Megen," I said, giving her a hug.

Careful not to get her hands on my shirt, she turned and gave me a big hug and kiss. Suddenly, she pulled back, looked me deeply in the eyes and asked, "Do you love you, Daddy?"

Astonished, I muttered, "Well...yes, Megen. I do love me."

"Good, then I know you love me," she said, settling back to work.

Now, remember, this is a five year old, not a psych major. I said to her, "Megen, where did you get that?"

Without batting an eye, she said, "Well, Dad, there is a girl in our class and she said that if you really love yourself then you can really love other people."

Misty-eyed, I gave her a big hug again, goopy hands and all. "Megen, that was really beautiful." In my mind I was thinking, *Out of the mouth of babes....*

Megen articulated an important concept. It is impossible to love other people, if you don't first love yourself. A good portion of loving yourself comes from the affirmation and encouragement from Dad.

When Dad Is Gone

A recent study discovered among adults today, twenty-three percent grew up without a father in the home. Twenty-nine percent grew up with a father who was physically present - -emotionally distant. Fifteen percent grew up with an abusive father. If we add up the totals, two-thirds of the adults in society today grew up without an involved, nurturing, affirming father.[2]

Is it any wonder, then, the anger we see in kids today? The emotional detachment and violence they see in their own homes is transferred to society at large through their actions. More and more children are killing children: teenagers are committing progressively violent crimes.

When affirmation and encouragement are missing during the early years of a child's development, inappropriate, anti-social behavior is, often, the result. Children do best when there is a father involved in their lives.

None of us was given an instruction manual when our children were born. We've had to pretty much "wing it" on our own. One of the resources we've used has been the example of our father. "If it was good enough for Dad, it's good enough for me." Unfortunately, too many fathers, grandfathers and great-grandfathers made some serious mistakes in their fathering.

Bad habits have a way of filtering down from generation to generation. Exodus 34:7 (NIV) speaks of "visiting the iniquity of the fathers upon the children and the children's children, to the third and fourth generation." If your father was a caring, nurturing dad who made you feel special and loved, by all means, emulate his example to the fullest! Most fathers are fallible humans. Emulate his best and avoid his worst.

Judging Your Father

Before you start to judge your father, it might be best to understand him. It's always easier to pick apart his shortcomings, document - - in detail - - his failures, dwell upon those times he let you down. But if you don't try to understand him, it'll be tough to forgive him.

Many of you reading this book had abusive or alcoholic fathers. Growing up was filled with pain and hurt. You may have a difficult time forgiving. Others will have grown up in a home where everyone just existed. Dad paid the bills, argued with Mom, had time for a few activities with the kids. You came through childhood relatively unscathed, but Dad simply wasn't involved much, emotionally.

If you are fortunate, you had a father who understood the nurturing process. Whether or not he had a good role model in his own dad; learned how to become a good father; or simply gave it his "best shot", most of the time he did it right.

Beware of becoming trapped in the "generation cycle." We parent the way we were parented. In order to break this cycle, I recommend parenting not only from an adult point of view, but also from a child's. When you think back to your father and how he parented you, remember how you felt about it. If he was a good parent and you felt great about yourself and your relationship with him, do the same with your own kids. If he left a lot to be desired as a parent, think back to what you would have liked from him as a child. Try to make sure you fill in those gaps with your own kids.

No father, however great, is perfect. Becoming a parent yourself causes you to consider the job your father did. He won't have done everything right. As much as possible, you need to celebrate his victories and forgive his failures.

How To Affirm

The positive affects of affirmation start early. Research shows that infants need the warm, caring touch of adults, preferably parents. Babies need to be held and cuddled. Lack of physical touch has caused a syndrome in children called "failure to thrive." Throughout childhood and into adult years, people have a continuing need for meaningful touch.

When John and Megen were little scrappers, we used to play a game called, "Brahma Bull." I was the bull, on my hands and knees on the living room floor. John and Megen were "bull-riders." Their job was to stay on the bull. My job was to "buck" them off.

We had times we wrestled on the carpet, played tackle football outside on the lawn, had piggyback rides to our hearts content. When Megen and I would go to the mall, we always held hands. It was our way of saying to ourselves and everyone we passed, "We belong together."

Hugs - The Miracle Medicine

Want to live longer? Guard against illness? Ward off depression and stress? Have a stronger family? Go to sleep without pills? Try hugging.

Studies have shown an interesting physical change when two people hug or touch each other. "The amount of hemoglobin in the blood increases significantly," says

Helen Colton, author of *The Gift of Touch*. "Hemoglobin is a part of the blood that carries vital supplies of oxygen to all organs of the body - including the heart and brain. An increase in hemoglobin tones up the whole body, and helps prevent heart disease and speeds recovery from illness."

The article goes on to say, "regular hugging can actually prolong life by curing harmful depression and stimulating a stronger will to live...The warm, meaningful embrace can have a very positive effect on people, particularly during times of widespread stress and tension like today."[3]

Hugs are great medicine to guard against the negative forces of this world!

Phrases That Encourage
"That's great."
"Good work!"
"That's a winner!"
"You can do it!"
"Fantastic!"
"Keep up the good work!"

Phrases That Stifle
"That's no good."
"That won't work."
"We've tried that before."
"That's not the way to do it."
"You just don't understand."
"Who do you think you are?"

The Words We Speak

Just as hugging is significant to our physical and emotional health, so are the words we speak to our children. Words can be "control buttons" because they tend to build up a person or break them down. A steady diet of negative words break down the spirit of a child.

Like the petal of a flower which opens when it's light, but closes when dark, so the spirit of a child opens up when affirmed, but closes when criticized.

I challenge you, fathers, to be men who choose words carefully, to build up your child's self-worth.

Affirming Others

Why is it that people outside the family are often treated with more affirmation than those inside the family? None of us would say they are more important than our own family. Erma Bombeck has a wonderful illustration:

"On TV, a child psychologist said parents should treat their children as they would treat their best friend - - with courtesy, dignity and diplomacy. *I have never treated my children any other way*, I told myself. But later that night I thought about it."

"Suppose our good friends, Fred and Eleanor, came to dinner, and ...."

"Well, it's about time you two got here! What have you been doing? Dawdling? Shut the door, Fred. Were you born in a barn? So Eleanor, how have you been? I've been meaning to have you over for ages..... Fred, take it easy on the chip and dip, or you'll ruin dinner...."
Heard from any of the gang lately? Got a card from the Martin's, they're in Lauderdale again....What's the matter, Fred? You're fidgeting. It's down the hall, first door on the left. And I don't want to see a towel in the middle fo the floor when you're finished!.....So, how are the children? If everybody's hungry, we'll go to dinner.

"You all wash up and I'll dish up the food....Don't tell me your hands are clean, Eleanor. I saw you playing with the dog!....Fred, you sit here and Eleanor, you sit here with the half glass of milk. You know, you're all thumbs when it comes to milk. Fred, I don't see any peas on your plate. You don't like peas? Have you ever tried them? Well, try a spoonful. If you don't like them, I won't make you eat them. But if you don't try it, you can forget dessert.

"Now what were we talking about? Oh yes, the Grubers. They sold their home and took a beating, but - - Eleanor, don't talk with food in your mouth. And use your napkin."

At that moment, in my fantasy, my son walked into the room. "How nice of you to come," I said pleasantly.

"Now what did I do?" he sighed.

*   *   *   *   *

Often, outsiders are treated with more courtesy and kindness than our children. Like Erma Bombeck's humorous solution, why don't we try treating our kids like our best friends.

Affirming Yourself

I think you've discovered you didn't always get all of the affirmation needed as children. You may also find you don't get all the affirmation you need for being dad. Now and then, your children may come forth with the words, "I love you, Dad." They may even come home with a school project crafted especially for you, even if it takes you a while to figure out exactly what it is. If you and your spouse are working as a team, you should receive affirmation from her.

If you don't think you're being affirmed enough, why not try affirming yourself? This can be very encouraging and not too difficult, with practice.

1. Thank You Lord, that I am created by You, and very special to You. (from Psalm 139:13-16)

2. Thank You Lord, that You have good plans for me. (Jeremiah 29:11-13)

3. Thank You Lord, that You have created me for good works. (Ephesians 2:10)

4. Thank You Lord, that I am in the process of becoming the person You want me to be, and the person I want to be.(Jeremiah 18:1-6)

Affirmation has great power in its effects, whether directed toward someone else or yourself. Something happens when we give our approval, by word or deed.

My mother always said, "Happiness is like a perfume. You cannot give it to others without getting a few drops on yourself."

THE BOTTOM LINE

Open your children up by the warmth of your words.

1. Can you recall a time when your father affirmed you? What did it feel like?

2. Why is it that many people are slow to affirm others.

3. In what ways do you affirm and/or encourage your children?

4. What are some creative ways you can do a better job of affirming your family?

Chapter Five......DAD THE HUSBAND

Loving Their Mother

The two swayed together, the only sound the rhythmic squeaking of the porch swing. No one said a word.

Finally, the man asked in exasperation, "What's wrong with you? You're as quiet as a tomb!"

The woman answered softly, "I was just thinking. . . you never tell me you love me any more."

"Look," the man told her sternly, "I told you I loved you the night we were married. If I ever change my mind, you'll be the first to know!"

* * * * *

Many books and articles are being written about families, marriage, fathers. I originally wanted to call the organization I started, *Dads and Kids*, instead of *Family Insights*. Something didn't quite seem to fit with that name, however. There was an ingredient missing. The missing ingredient was *Mom*.

In America today, nineteen million children live with only their mothers. Among children of divorce, forty percent won't even see their father in a typical year.[1] With the epidemic absence of fathers in the lives of America's children, it is often mothers who hold family units together.

"The glory of children is in their fathers, (Proverbs 17:6 NIV)" the saying may go, but mothers are the tender, loving, and caring ingredient who make the family complete. Any relationship you have with your children will be affected by your relationship with their mother.

This chapter will focus primarily on the husband-wife relationship, those marriages which are still intact. The information will still be useful for divorced spouses. However different the paths of divorced parents, they will be linked together by their children. *In other words, even though she is no longer your wife, she will always be their mother.*

Not everything in this chapter will apply to divorced parents, but the concepts can be modified to bring insight on getting along with a divorced spouse.

The Best Gift A Father Can Give

How would you complete this sentence: The best gift a father can give to his children is _____? You might want to fill in the blank with: "Spend time with them" , "Love them" , "Get involved in sports with them", "Listen to them", "Be there for them." All of these would be useful in building positive relationships with your children.

This, however, is how I would phrase that statement: The best gift a father can give to his children is *to love their mother.* Most men probably would respond, "Hey! I already do that!"

A few years ago, my father and I were driving home from a baseball game. It was one of those special times when we felt comfortable with each other. Dad seemed willing to share a little more than usual.

"I sure am lucky," he told me.

"Why do you think you're lucky, Dad?"

"I've been married to your mother for over fifty years," he said. "I sure am a lucky man."

I agreed, of course, then after a moment I asked, "Did you ever tell her that, Dad?"

"Oh, Terry, she knows!" he replied, exasperated.

I paused a minute. "You know, Dad, Mom needs to hear that often. She needs to know how you feel about her. Every woman needs to know they are loved and appreciated."

"Terry," he said, curtly, "I said, she knows. I've told her before!"

End of conversation. We rode the rest of the way home in silence.

* * * * *

I'm not sure you can tell someone too often you love them, whether it's your wife or your kids. Daily, we are all bombarded with messages that we're not good enough . From the television we hear we're not thin enough, don't use the right product, aren't rich enough. On the road, we get honked at for going too slow, and a ticket for going too fast. At work or at school, everything we do is looked at, evaluated and , in most cases, criticized. There should always be a place, a relationship, a refuge from the world's bruises, where we can go to get built-up, where people will say, "I love you. You're important to me." That place, that relationship, that refuge is the family.

All relationships within the family affect each other. When children know their father and mother have a good relationship, they feel secure. No matter what happens outside the walls of the family, inside children feel safe. The cornerstone of that wall-of-security is the positive relationship between "Mom and Dad." Children know they are a part of both parents. When those parents are in harmony, the child feels secure.

Because of the love which exists between parent and child, the opinions and judgments of the parent are often mirrored by the child. There is a shared sense of value. Parents pass on many of their own attitudes and opinions to their children. The children take "ownership" of those ideas. It is very difficult for children, especially young children, to deal with a fundamental difference in how they see something and how a parent sees it.

Let me put it this way: Johnny loves Mommy. Johnny loves Daddy. Johnny doesn't understand why Daddy doesn't love Mommy. There can't be something wrong with Mommy, because Johnny loves Mommy. There can't be something wrong with Daddy, because Johnny loves Daddy. There must be something wrong with Johnny.

When relationships in a family are not functioning smoothly, tension is produced. Children often will internalize that tension, viewing themselves as the cause.

When Daddy loves Mommy, the gift of security is given, as well as the gift of affirmation. The wisdom of the child - - in loving their mother - - is affirmed by the father's love of his wife. Father and child are in agreement. Harmony and security are established.

Since this relationship between mother and father is so important to the emotional stability of children, how can fathers take the lead in establishing and maintaining it?

The Nurturing Process

The key word in a marriage relationship is nurturing. Nurturing is essentially *nourishing*. When we nurture another person, we help them to grow. Nurturing is that thoughtful deed or kind word which builds up another. Nurturing is being available to the other person during difficult times, to listen, to advise, to hold.

I am told that approximately 80% of all books on family matters are bought by women. Most men simply do not spend much time dealing with the subject. Women seem to be much more attuned to the needs of the family and motivated to try and do something about them. Men seem more content to exist within the status quo. One might conclude, men just aren't good nurturers.

However, men are very good at nurturing, in the initial stage of courtship. Remember the cards and letters to her? The phone calls, just to "see how you're doing?" The walks along the beach, the "just-plain-being-together" time? During the courtship phase, most men can be very romantic, nurturing the fragile relationship.

So what happened to "....and they lived happily ever after?" Best-selling author, Gary Smalley, explains it this way: Once men get to the altar, they tend to feel they have conquered.[2] In essense, the "chase" is over. Most men turn their "conquering attention" to jobs or other pursuits. They move on to the next "challenge."

Over the years, as work commitments increase for both husband and wife, and as children arrive on the scene, the daily routine becomes predictable. Husband and wife see less and less of each other in those roles, exclusively. Energies are taken up being "worker," "boss," "Mommy," or "Daddy." The special chemistry and bond of "husband" and "wife" begins to wane. Eventually, mom and dad can end up "just existing."

Communication Patterns

Over the years, I've seen a pattern develop in many marriages. There is a chart I've created showing this pattern (see page 63). At the top of the triangle, notice how close the husband and wife are. This represents the wedding day, the bond of togetherness. The two-way arrow in the middle of the triangle represents either the emotional closeness or distance between husband and wife. As the months and years go on, the couple builds a communication pattern with each other.

On the left is the nurturing process. This takes a good deal of effort and creativity to maintain during the life of a marriage. Even though I considered myself a "good" husband, my lack of nurturing led to a divorce with my first wife. I have since learned how important it is to maintain special times of fun and romance which re-ignite intimacy and closeness.

On the right is an abusive pattern. Unfortunately, some men fall into this category. Often they repeat the pattern they saw with their own parents. Verbal abuse, physical abuse, controlling, or neglecting a spouse are potent patterns which must be consciously fought against. If this has been the pattern you grew up with, and find yourself perpetuating, it is vital for all your relationships to seek help in changing.

Most couples, I've found, fall somewhere in the middle. I refer to this as "just existing." The husband and wife begin to take each other for granted. Generally speaking, *He* gets locked into work, sports, hobbies, his buddies. *She* begins to find her enjoyment in work, shopping, hobbies, taking care of the house and the kids.

Eventually, the communication declines. They realize their lives have little in common. Both feel the other is taking them for granted. Their lives become predictable, their marriage unexciting. Looking at the chart, you'll notice being taken for granted leads to a lack of feeling. The emotional side of the relationship, which once was filled with romance, trust and intimacy, has now turned to numbness.

As numbness takes over, distance is built. What used to be a spontaneous gift of a card or flower, now turns into a routine duty at a birthday or anniversary. As the distance gets larger, the barriers grow higher. The farther the two grow apart, the sooner one partner will want out of the relationship. Emotional separation, or actual divorce, will follow.

During this time of distance, numbness and neglect, children get caught in the middle. Sensitive to the moods of their parents, but unable to understand the adult nuances of their parents' behavior, children are left poorly equipped to interpret and deal with these patterns.

The "Just Existing" Pattern

Often we get into this pattern without realizing it. It's hard to get out of where you are, if you don't know how you got there. To further illustrate how couples get into this "just existing" pattern, I've found it useful in my counseling to have a chart (see page 64). As the misunderstandings and miscommunication between husband and wife continue, conflicts increase. Conflicts produce tension and stress for everyone in the family. Eventually, the husband and wife relationship begins to deteriorate. Unless the couple chooses to work at rebuilding the relationship, the only alternatives are to severe the relationship or to simply exist together, enduring over the years.

Whose Problem Is It?

When I was growing up, my parents sought a divorce. Back then, there had to be "grounds." After they had been living apart for nearly a year, the judge decided there were no grounds and refused to grant the divorce.

"You two go home and start working it out!" he ordered my parents. Dad moved back into the house.

Years later, when I was involved in a marriage and family counseling practice, I asked my dad about that time apart from us.

"You know, Dad," I said, "When you were out of the house, what did you see as the problem between you and Mom?"

Without hesitation, he said, "I never could figure out your Mother's problem!" As far as he was concerned, it was Mom's problem.

He's right. It was Mom's problem. But it was his problem too! Even though they endured fifty-two years of marriage, too much of the time was spent "just existing" together. It wasn't good for Mom, for Dad, for my brothers or for me.

Perhaps the question shouldn't be, "Who's problem is it?" but rather, "Who's solution is it?" or "Let's work on the solution, together."

Choosing To Make Changes

A marriage or relationship allowed to slip into the "just existing" pattern doesn't have to remain. If you perceive your marriage to have fallen into this dead-end rut, make a decision to do everything you can to change it. First, you'll need to determine areas to make changes in. I know it would be easier to determine areas where *she* needs to make changes, but initially the only person you can really change is yourself. If you aren't sure where to start, I've outlined a few areas to start improving your relationship.

Time and Energy   One of the first areas to begin with is how you divide up your time and energy.

In writing this book, I asked a lot of students and adults about their fathers. One of the questions I asked was a fill-in-the-blank. "If there was one thing I wish my father had done differently, it would be _____." Predictably, many of the responses I got back were, "Dad, I wish you would have spent more time with me."

However, several responses had to do with another member of the family.

"Dad, I wish you would have treated Mom better."

"Dad, I wish you would have spent more time with Mom."

Wives and children can feel they're getting the leftovers from the man of the house. Whatever is left after work or other activities they get. They feel everything, and everyone else, is more important.

One insightful young man summed it up with, "I wish my father would have been more perceptive to my mother's needs."

Being perceptive takes time: time to be around the person to know what their needs are. Being perceptive to needs is not enough. Once needs are perceived, there should be an attempt to fill those needs. Filling needs takes energy. Time and energy. Begin to incorporate these elements into your family relationships.

Regaining The Intimate Touch   That which is conquered can always be lost. Therefore, I encourage couples to get back into the courting mode. Women can be romantic, requiring an element of courting to continue in marriage. Through word and deed, your wife needs to know she is appreciated and high on your priority list.

Don't forget the power of touch! "Touching base" with your wife through the day, by placing a note where she'll find it, making a quick phone call on a break, or physically touching her when you get home, reaffirms the promise of an intimate and close relationship.

Building A Team Effort   Men love sports. We love to be on, and root for, a team. The most important team you'll ever be a part of, the most important team you can ever root for, is your family. Your wife and children need to know they're part of your team.

Children who have a father who treats his wife with dignity, respect, kindness and loving concern are very fortunate indeed. In return, the wife can be a great blessing to her husband, as she encourages him in his pursuits. Not only does the marriage become a team effort, but children will have a good role model in how to treat a woman properly. Security and emotional stability will reign in the home.

The world of a child is full of emotional bumps and bruises. Home needs to be safe place. Children won't soon forget how Dad's love for Mom made them feel.

THE BOTTOM LINE

The best gift a father can give his children, is to love their mother.

Five Ways I Can Improve My Relationship with Their Mom.

1._____

2._____

3._____

4._____

5._____

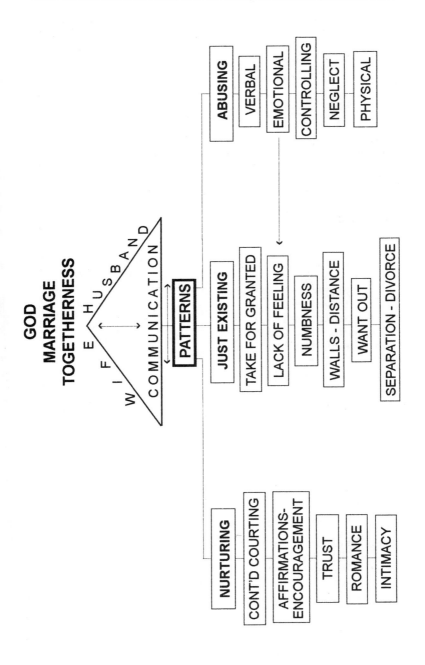

You Just Don't Understand!!

Communication Breakdown
Between Husband and Wife

SHE.........	HE.........
Feels she carries most of the load; works outside the home, does housework, cooks, manages kids.	Feels he carries financial burden for the family plus yard work, home duties, car repairs.
Feels like home actvities keep her exhausted.	Watches television alot. Big on sports page of newspaper.
Needs courting, affirmations, romance, and encouragement.	Tends to forget about or neglect nurturing.
Feels everything and everyone else is more important than she is and she expresses this to him...	Is unsure how to meet her needs. Feels like whatever he tries isn't good enough. Feels inadequate.
Feels frustrated with the relationship. Concentrates more and more effort on the kids, job, etc.	Frustrated because she's not as interested in sex as he is.
Begins to feel she's "just existing" in the relationship. Walls begin to come up.	Does his own thing. Minimal effort put into the home and their relationship.
Suggests they get counseling.	Says, "Go ahead. It's your problem, not mine."
Feels numbness set in. Begins thinking of leaving.	Emotionally disconnected from her. May be verbally abusive in frustration.
Feels emotional distance is deepening. Begins seriously thinking of leaving.	Is "just existing." Is cool and distant towards her.
Informs husband she "wants out."	Realizes he is no longer in control. Suggests counseling.
Responds with, "Too late!"	Is devastated. Can't understand how they got this way.

Chapter Six......DAD THE FRIEND

Building the Bridges of Friendship

*"Friendship," said Christopher Robin, "is a very comforting sort of thing." A.A. Milne in **Winnie The Pooh***

Friendship is...
...one of the most treasured gifts in life, given from one person to another.
...high praise for the one who receives it.
...a gift all admire and long to experience.
...essential to a life lived well.
...often as elusive as it is essential.

Great literature is full of stories about friendship; Tom Sawyer and Huckleberry Finn, Mowgli and Baloo, the sisters in Little Women. One of the oldest and most respected books ever written, the Bible, has many stories of friendship. My favorite story is found in the Old Testament. It is the story of Jonathan and David.

Shortly after David was victorious in battle over Goliath, the Philistine, David was brought before Saul, King of Israel. While meeting Saul was a great honor, David experienced something of even greater value. He met Jonathan, Saul's son. The two became fast friends.

Their camaraderie is described in this way, "After David had finished talking with Saul, Jonathan became one in spirit with David, and he loved him as he loved himself...And Jonathan made a covenant with David because he loved him as himself." (I Samuel 18:1-3 NIV)

Their friendship, however fast, wasn't easy. King Saul became jealous of David and sought ways to kill him. Jonathan often found himself in a position of protecting his friend, thus going against his father's will. Through their struggles together, Jonathan and David forged a chemistry of togetherness, a camaraderie of heart-touching-heart, a friendship without limit.

This is exactly the type of friendship your children want with their father.

Special Time With Dad

I can still remember waiting for my dad to come home. It was especially hard during the summer months, without school to take up time. I'd spend my days with friends, often at the ballfield near our house, or riding bikes. As soon as the sun began to set, I knew it was time for dad to be come home.

I couldn't wait for dinner to be over so we could go out on the sidewalk and throw the ball to each other. It was important for me to know, with everything else my dad had to do, he still could find time for me.

When my own children were small, I couldn't wait to open the door to our house. A shrill, little voice would yell out, "Daddy's home!" as if those were the most important words in the world. To Megen and John, they were.

Most of us dads don't realize the significance those early years with our children are until they are much older. If we could recognize how crucial those years of three to eleven are, we'd probably work extra hard at fathering.

Father/Daughter

You're the first man your daughter will ever love. You're the first man to ever love her. The love you give her will help her to know she can be loved by another. These elements comprise the special relationship between father and daughter.

With a son, dads look to themselves. They see themselves in the man their son will become. Often, father and son will have a different vision of who that man should be. There is almost a built-in competitiveness fathers and sons need to deal with. Sons use their fathers as a benchmark to gauge their own manhood.

Daughters need their fathers in a different way. There is a vacumn in the heart of a daughter only her father can fill. In my years of counseling, I've never gotten over the pain in an adult woman's life if her relationship with her father is damaged. No matter how old she becomes, the little-girl longing for daddy to love her just never seems to go away. I have seen women engage in destructive attempts to fill that void. Promiscuity, depression, eating disorders are strategies I've seen used to numb the pain of a "daddy-void."

Unconditional love and acceptance provides your daughter with security as she is growing up. You are her "champion," ready to take on all-comers to protect her. This allows her the security to venture out on her own.

However, if dad is not emotionally or physically available to his daughter, she will look elsewhere. School hallways and mall walkways are full of young men who gladly will fill the emotional needs of "vulnerable" young girls. If you aren't available to give her the approval and affirmation she needs, one of them will. He'll provide her with the male friendship she's been needing. Unfortunately, he may ask a price to providing "friendship." Too many times I have seen sexual promiscuity the result of a daughter's desperate attempt to find a man to love her.

I have written about this in the previous chapter, but I will caution again. Be aware of how you are treating her mother. From your treatment, your daughter will draw conclusions about how men do, and should, treat women. Ask yourself a question: "Would I want a man treating my daughter like I treat her mother?" Remember, your opinions and actions are important to your daughter. She watches what you do. She may very well end up marrying someone like "dear, old dad."

In the United States, one million teenage girls will become pregnant this year alone. Of the nearly 2,800 pregnancies a day, 365 will end in miscarriage. Over one-thousand will end in an abortion. The rest of the pregnancies will result in children being born. Tomorrow another 2,800 girls will become pregnant.[1] In the past, we have dismissed these teenage girls as "boy crazy." Many of them are "crazy", desperately looking for a father's love in all the wrong places.

It doesn't need to be this way. By starting now, while your daughter is young, you can provide her with the positive male role-model she needs in her life. Building a friendship with your daughter, now, can help her bridge the chasm into womanhood.

Though it is always best to start young, it's never too late to start. As I've said, I've seen too many adult women with child-size holes in their hearts where "Daddy" should be. It will take more of an effort on your part, but I urge fathers with daughters of all ages to reach out to them. You might be amazed to discover you're still her "first love."

A Father and Son

Who taught you to drive your first car? Start the power mower? Change the oil in the crankcase? Handle a gun? Pound a nail? Saw a board? Fix a flat tire? In most cases, the answer will be "My dad." Dad becomes the role model in a thousand-and-one life situations. From these, children learn how to deal with life. From these, sons learn how to be a man.

From fathers, daughters learn how to operate *around* a man. Sons learn how to operate *as* a man. They will observe how you react in any number of given situations and file your reactions away. Taken together, these reactions build a picture of "manhood." Because children aren't always aware of the real reasons why you react in certain ways, it is important to talk to them about how you're feeling, what you're doing and why. This doesn't have to be a stern father-son conference like Ward and Beaver Cleaver used to have on *"Leave It To Beaver."* You can teach your son, your daughters too, in every day life situations.

Games of Bonding "For most of us, our father was our first coach," wrote a sports columnist in an article published on Father's Day. "Games bind fathers and kids together for a lifetime."[2]

This writer went on to mirror something that was certainly true for many boys: "There was a time when the most important thing in my life was the game of catch after dinner. My father taught me how to ride a bike and how to swim. He taught me how to shoot a jumper and how to make a pivot on a double play."[3]

Was that sports writer talking about just games? No, through games dads teach kids how to win and lose in life.

Beyond the lessons learned, through playing games, is the sheer joy of being together. It needn't be outside games, it can be inside games also. I started out sitting with my children and putting together puzzles. We'd talk about the farm scene or the family or the cars and trucks as they took shape under our hands. Later, we worked on math through counting games, flash cards or a game of Yahtzee. Finally, there was the time they could handle the concentration necessary for a game of checkers. Through all of these, we'd talk about the game, their life, my life, school, whatever. And we'd be together.

The Need for Dad's Approval

My father's last days were lived out in a convalescent home, where he could get constant care for Lou Gehrig's disease. One sunny September afternoon, I came to visit and push his wheelchair around the flowered grounds of the home. It was pleasant and warm, the sweet smell of the blossoms mingling with moist, freshly cut grass. A lazy sort of afternoon and Dad and I were talking, as we usually did, about sports. Toward the end of our walk, I suddenly felt I had to let him know something.

"Dad," I said, "I want to thank you for being a good dad. You provided for us boys (there were three of us). You were always encouraging us in sports."

It felt good to finally tell him straight-out. His answer wasn't what I expected. "It wasn't always easy," he said.

The more I thought about his answer, the more I realized how much I'd wanted him to say something else. I wanted him to say something like, "Thanks for being a good son, Terry. I was always proud of you." I so wanted to hear his approval for me, for my chosen profession, for my life.

Every time I talked about my work, my ministry and counseling, he was always negative. It hurt for him to be critical of me as a child, and it still hurt to have him withhold his approval as an adult. When we'd talk, I'd leave determined to show him how well I could do, no matter how old I was.

My father is deceased, but before he died I feel I was able to forgive him. Still, I wish I could have shared some of my feelings. There was a part of me I never felt safe sharing with him. I was intimidated by his controlling and critical nature. I was always afraid of being rejected so there were many subjects I just avoided. Because I wasn't able to share myself with my dad, we never reached the level of friendship and camaraderie I wish we could have. I forgive my dad, but I'll always miss what might have been.

After my father died, my mother told me something that put many things about dad into perspective. She told my brothers and me our father didn't really want to have children. Learning that helped me understand why my father hadn't ever worked at being my best friend.

I feel much of my desire to be involved in the lives of children, to provide help for families trying to survive in this world, is because of my father. While I loved and forgave him, I didn't want to be like him. I wanted to learn how to do better. As I studied and worked through my own life, it seemed natural to share what I'd learned with others. I've tried to take from my dad the good things he did, the good times we shared, and build on them.

Looking back on my own experience as a father, through what I've learned and studied for counseling, several keys elements to being your child's friend become clear.

Choosing To Be Good Friends

Friendships don't just happen. They are the result of conscious decision. It doesn't matter what age your children are at this moment, make a conscious choice to reach out to them. Be their friend, even if they sometimes give you fits!

Being their friend doesn't mean you have to act like Santa Claus 365 days a year. In your role as father, it will be necessary for you to discipline your children. Sometimes this can be the highest act of love. Children need limits and boundaries to function. This is not only so they aren't injured, but also to give them a sense of security.

When a good foundation of friendship is established, there is less need for discipline. Your child will value the friendship they have with you and won't want to jeopardize it by continual disobedience. Of course, every child will disobey, but even in discipline your love and friendship can be conveyed.

By being your child's friend, you also will be giving them the proper pattern for friendships in later life.

> A friend is someone who is *Faithfully there, through the good and bad times.*
>
> A friend is honest and *Real with emotions and thoughts.*
>
> A friend is *Involved with you, spends time with you.*
>
> A friend is *Encouraging. Seeks to build you up, not tear you down.*
>
> A friend *Needs and allows you to provide for their needs.*
>
> A friend *Demonstrates love through word and deed.*

Building Closeness Through Affirmation

One of the biggest bridge-builders in friendship is affirmation. Praise and encouragement go much farther to motivate than criticism and being negative. Your children need to know your love for them doesn't end when they make a mistake. Affirmation is the glue that holds friendships together. (Remember Chapter Four: DAD THE ENCOURAGER)

Building Communication Through Approval

The opposite of an affirming attitude is being judgmental. The words you use to communicate to your children are very important. Continual put-downs erode the spirit of your child.

Your approval is constantly sought by your children. If you make a habit of responding with the messages like, "Why can't you do anything right?!" this bridge will be burned. Your children will distance themselves from you and build walls between you.

Hollywood comedian, Don Rickles, has made a living out of sarcastic, stinging humor. His routine is one snide remark, caustic put-down or cheap shot, after another. As funny as he may be to begin with, after a while he starts to wear pretty thin. Our children don't need a "Don Rickles" in the house. A steady diet of judgmental statements and sarcasm from us will leave them deflated. Divisiveness, not closeness, will be the inevitable result.

This caution to avoid put-down statements needs to extend not only to your children but to those your children look up to. It may be a celebrity who has caught their eye.

I have a friend whose daughter became enamored with a rock star. This wasn't the sort of person her father was thrilled about. He didn't approve of his lifestyle, dress or attitude. Instead of being critical of her infatuation, though, he chose to take "the high road." He learned all he could about this person, listened to his music, and showed an interest in his concerts. He'd make sure to tell his daughter whenever this rock star appeared on television or sung on the radio. It didn't take too long for his daughter to lose interest!

It's very easy for us as parents to be critical of our children's choices. We care about the direction they're going in and, at times, worry about "negative influence."

As our children grow older and seek independence, we should find ways to influence them without demeaning their choices, curiousity and interests.

Rock stars are here one day and gone tomorrow. You, Dad, will always be their hero!

Building Trust Through Confronting

Recently, Megen told me about a conversation she'd had with her friend and her friend's father. Because of what I do, the subject of fathering came up. Parents and parental discipline quickly became the topic of discussion.

"I always know when my dad's really upset with me," Megen interjected, confidently. No doubt her friend's father was interested to hear how Megen knew.

"I know when he's really upset at me," my daughter told them, "because that's when he *doesn't* get mad at me." Her friend's father looked perplexed. She went on to explain, "Instead of getting mad at me, my dad gets very still and says in a calm voice, 'Megen, I need some help in understanding why this happened....' Then I know he's *really* mad!"

There are times when our children will do things that upset us. Rather than responding with, "Well, *that* was a stupid thing to do!" or lashing out in anger by yelling and berating their behavior, how about finding out what happened?

First of all, by putting the "ball" back in their court, you force them to explain their actions. It also gives you time to take a couple of deep breaths and calm down. Instead of telling your child, at the top of your lungs, why their behavior was wrong, this question allows all of you to do a couple of things. First, their explanation might correct a misunderstanding you have. Even fathers have been known to jump to a conclusion, now and again. Secondly, this approach can give your child an understanding of why their behavior was wrong without you having to say a word. Kids are pretty smart. They know a "lame" excuse when they hear one, especially one that's come out of their mouths!

True, you may need to take some sort of corrective measure, but the relationship hasn't been sent out-of-whack because you're bigger, louder, or can win through intimidation. The next time one of your kids does something you feel is out of line, try saying, "I need some help understanding why this happened." Like Megen, they may still know you're upset, but you'll give them the opportunity to explain. That's a courtesy most of us want when confronted.

Surprise! Building Closeness Through the Unexpected

As a single parent, I was always worried about my kids' eating. I fretted about everything being "nutritionally correct." Usually I made them a hot breakfast and a healthy lunch to take to school. I continued doing this, even when John was in high school.

One morning, we were all running late. John was hurriedly finishing his breakfast and I was slapping lunches together as fast as I could. Often in their lunches, I'd include carrot or celery sticks and hope they didn't get traded for Ding-Dongs!

Running out of time, I said to John, "I don't have time to slice the carrot up, just make sure you chew it up good!" (I have no idea why I said this to a teenager, perhaps it was momentary insanity, the rush of the morning.)

John gave me a look that said, *Get a grip, Dad.* Laughing out loud he said, "What did you think I would do, Dad? Swallow it whole?"

Kiddingly, I responded, "Sure! You football players are tough! I'll bet you even chew nails!"

John finished his breakfast and hustled down the hall to blow dry his hair. I slipped out into the garage and picked out five long nails. Hurrying back into the house while he couldn't see me, I placed them in a ziplock baggie and stuck them down in the brown paper sack with the rest of his lunch.

It was hard to contain my laughter as I thought about John, sitting around with his football buddies at lunch. "Hey, guys!" I could almost hear one of them say, "Look at this! John's dad feeds him nails!"

When John came home at 6:00 that evening after practice, I was in the kitchen making dinner. Carrying his gym bag, he leaned his head around the corner and smiled. "Thanks, Dad," he said, before heading up to his room. Later on, we both had a good laugh over the nails.

* * * * *

Little surprises, no matter how off-the-wall, help build closeness. They're like a shared secret or a private joke.

Everyone can identify with that inevitable question kids have when you return home from a vacation or business trip: "What did you bring me?" People love surprises, especially when least expected.

When Megen was in junior high and high school, I made it a point to mail her a card every now and then or bring her a flower. These surprises were special to her and I would often find that Teddy Bear card I sent tacked up on her wall near her bed.

As important as it is to verbally tell our children we love them, another way is to express that love through an unexpected action. "Surprise!" is another way of saying "I love you!"

The Value of Touch

I've talked about this in Chapter Four, but I want to reiterate how important touch is. Friendships are enhanced by touching, as are our emotional and physical health. Security for a child is wound up in the warmth of a caring embrace.

There is often confusion among dads about hugging or touching their daughters affectionately, especially as she begins to mature. Dads refrain from any physical contact, lest they be suspected of inappropriate touching or "molestation." Likewise, sons as they get older, may feel they have "out-grown" hugs from dad. A hug or kiss from dad puts their own emerging manliness in jeopardy.

It is important for you to be aware of how your child is feeling. Not everyone will react alike or consistently. In adolescence, they may want to be treated as an adult one day, and a child the next.

HUGS ARE......
Practically Perfect
Low Energy Consumption
High Energy Yield
No Monthly Payments
Non-Fattening
Inflation Proof
No Additives
No Preservatives
Non-Taxable
Non-Polluting
FULLY RETURNABLE

Don't make the mistake of dealing with this contradiction by stopping physical contact with your children altogether. For your daughter, perhaps a hug side-by-side would be better received than the full facing hug you did when she was younger. For your son, try a pat on the back or a shoulder squeeze, while still getting in that hug.

Physical touching is tangible affection. The days of grabbing up your child and smothering their neck with rasberries leave as they grow older. Pats on the back, a hand on the arm, a kiss on the cheek and, especially, a hug should never go out of style.

The Biggest Bridge of All

"When I'm talking with my dad, he's totally focused on me," I once heard a girl say. "If someone walks into the room, his eyes stay on me. He listens to me." She was telling one of the things she liked best about her father. I wish all fathers understood how important listening is to their children!

The analogy goes, "We have two ears and one mouth. We should do twice as much listening as talking!"

Most students I know say their dad really doesn't listen to them. I'm sure if you asked the father, most of them would say they are listening. What they view as listening and what their child views as listening are two different things. The best example I've seen for this is a poem I found called, *"Please Just Listen."*

When I ask you to listen to me and you start
  giving advice, you haven't done what I asked.
When I ask you to listen to me and you begin to
  tell me why I shouldn't feel that way,
  you're tramping on my feelings.
When I ask you to listen to me and you feel you
  have to do something to solve my problem

you've failed me....as strange as that may
seem.
Please listen! All I asked was that you listen,
not talk...or do.....just hear.[4]

Children just want us to hear them, first. After we have done that, there will be time for handing out advice, working through the feelings, or coming up with a solution. It all starts with our listening. While they talk and we listen, our child can take their own advice, work through their own feelings or come up with a solution on their own. Often our role is to provide a place for them to bounce ideas off of, not ram our ideas down their throats.

Decoding The Message

Sometimes, talking with another person is like decoding a secret language. In order for real communication to take place, you need to hear beyond the words to the feelings behind them. Their words may be saying, "Apple," but with your handy-dandy decoder ring, you realize what they really mean is, "Orange." It's no wonder words without feelings is like "talking apples and oranges."

A wife says to her husband, "Honey, we need to talk..."

"What's the matter?" he asks. "Is the washer still acting up?"

The husband is thinking something needs to be fixed. The wife simply wants some time to talk, without a specific purpose in mind.

*   *   *   *   *

A little child runs along the sidewalk. All of a sudden, he trips and falls, crying over a skinned knee. Dad comes up and yells, "Come on, get up! We'll wipe the blood off. You'll be fine. Stop that crying. Be a big boy!" The child only cries louder.

Mom comes up, puts her arm around him and says, "That must really hurt!" The child sniffles twice, then stops crying.

Dad offered advice. He told the child how to fix it. Mom assured the child his feelings were valid. Feeling validated, the child no longer needed to cry.

* * * * *

Learning to decode feelings doesn't happen overnight. It is a learned skill. Another way of saying "decode feelings" might be "active listening." It's not enough to hear the words, feel the feelings. You'll be surprised how well you can relate to those in your family, when you work on this skill.

Listening well is an important bridge of friendship. It's worth your effort.

Special Times Together

The key to building any friendship is time spent together. So it is with our children. They long to do things with their father. Many dads need ideas of things to do. Here are a few suggestions. Some are simple, others will take planning.

Fishing	See the Circus
Read a Story	Swim
Go for a Walk	Ride a Ferry
Bake Cookies	Ride Bikes
Wrestle on the floor	Play a Board Game
Take in a Movie	Go Shopping
Go out for a Meal	Play Par 3 Golf
Take a Day Hike	Go to the Park
Go for a Train Ride	Go Rollerblading
Visit an Airport	Play Ball

Visit the Science Center	Throw a Frisbee
Go Camping	Go to the Zoo
Go to the Beach	Go to Aquarium
Try a Trolley Ride	See a Ballgame
Roast Hot Dogs	Go Skiing
Fly Kites	Visit a Gym
Work a Puzzle	Go Ice Skating
Bathe the Dog	Play Ping Pong
Eat lots of Pizza	Take a Vacation

Building Friendship Around God

One of the best ways to build friendship with your children is to read stories to them. I enjoyed reading my children stories using a Children's Bible. I stumbled onto this when John and Megen were young. Every other evening we would sit together on the floor and read Bible stories. On the other days, we read from different children's books.

When we finished with a story, we'd join hands and each of us would say a short prayer. We'd try to stress thankfulness in our prayers instead of "wantfulness." We'd thank God for each other, for our family, for what we already had.

Several years later, when John was about to graduate from high school, I took him aside and said, " John, I'm very proud of you. You've done well in high school. My only regret, as a dad, is that I haven't been able to provide you with a lot of the things your friends have." (I was thinking of his own car so he could drive to school, a large and fancy home to live in, ski vacations, that sort of thing.)

John responded with, "Don't worry about it, Dad. I'm a lot better off because I haven't had everything."

The seeds of John's response were planted early, on the floor together, during those friendship-building years. Today, both children exhibit a thankfulness for life and don't seemed overly concerned about material possessions. They possess many things, but their things don't seem to possess them.

More importantly, they seem secure in who they are and in the meaning they find in life. The truth is, children don't need a lot of "things" to be happy, they just need a lot of "you," Dad.

THE BOTTOM LINE

The best friend your child will ever have is you.

1. In what ways did your father befriend you?

2. What could he have done to insure a deeper friendship with you?

3. In what ways do you see yourself building a friendship with your children?

4. If you were to ask your children, how would they see you as their friend?

Now, ask your children and see what they say!!

Chapter Seven......DAD THE FAITHFUL

Following Through With Your Promises

Marge was busy cleaning up the dinner dishes, when the phone rang. She waited for it to ring twice, hoping one of the kids would pick it up. When it continued to ring, she dried her soap-lathered hands and ran to catch it.

"Hello?" she said, slightly out of breath.

"Hello, Marge. It's Jim." Her stomach sank. It was her ex-husband's weekend to take the kids. When she didn't say anything, he continued, "Marge, I can't make it over this weekend. Would you tell Josh and Sarah something's come up? I can't see them."

She tried not to let disappointment overwhelm her. "They were really looking forward to this weekend with you," she explained slowly. "You promised you'd take them to the beach on Sunday."

"Look, just tell them I can't make it and I'll make it up to them," he responded, tersely. "I'm sure they'll understand."

"I'm not sure I do," she told him. "I made plans this weekend, expecting them to be with you."

"I'm sorry, Marge, but it can't be helped. Just tell them for me, okay? Thanks." He hung up before she could say anything else. Taking a deep breath to calm herself, she struggled to think what she would tell the kids.

* * * * *

Most of us can remember a time when we were excited about something special about to happen: a long awaited vacation, a visit from a friend, a lucrative business trip, an expected promotion at work, or a holiday off. We thought about it for days, maybe even weeks. We planned what we'd do and dreamed about how it would feel. We eagerly anticipated that special event happening.

Now, remember a time when what you were expecting didn't happen. The disappointment and let-down are hard to forget.

Eager anticipation is just how a child feels when looking forward to time with Dad. Just to be with Dad is pretty special, but even more so when it's to take a hike, ride a train, or go to the beach. Whatever the situation, a child longs to spend time with Dad. They may not say so, but the feeling is real.

A while back, I spoke primarily to men who were still married. This chapter will most often deal with divorced men, fathers who are away from their children. I asked the divorced dads to try and take what they could out of Chapter Five. Now, it's time for the still-at-home fathers to try and take what they can out of this chapter. If you're living at home, the concepts of keeping your promise and spending special time with your children is something you need to hear. The situations described may not necessarily apply, but the principles behind them certainly do.

One of the strongest disappointments for children is when their father can't spend promised time with them. Whether dad is living at home or away, the terrible let-down of a promise broken lingers in the heart of a child.

The Pain of Abandonment

Children trust our promises. If we promise to be with them and aren't, for whatever reason, our children feel abandoned. Jim didn't stop to realize the effect on Marge or his children. Marge had to rearrange plans, and the children spent the weekend sulking in their rooms, full of disappointment. Every broken promise, every outing missed, every day wasted etches indelible memories into a child's mind.

Kids, especially young ones, can't comprehend prior commitments, work pressures, or changing your mind. The fact you don't show up tells them only one thing: you don't want to be with them. They'll assume they aren't important enough or good enough to spend time with you. They'll assume you just don't care.

Jim might decide to make up for his failure to show by bringing gifts next time he does see his children. A game, a doll or a bat will get him off the hook, he'll figure. He's figuring wrong. Children want your presence, not your presents!

When Hurt Turns To Anger

Imagine how a child feels when he or she finds out Dad stood them up for a day at the office, a new girlfriend, or a round of golf with his buddies. The excuse of "something's come up" just doesn't cut-it. If a father bows out too often, the child's feels rejected and angry. Seeds of disappointment grow into bitterness.

Like the song, *Cats In The Cradle*, I mentioned before, time denied your children now can become time denied you later. During their teenage years, when they are able to express their independence, don't be surprised if they don't have much time for you. You might be tempted to think they are being disrespectful, or even standoffish. It may simply be their way of saying, "You weren't there for me when I needed you. I had to learn to get along in life without you, and I have. I don't have time for you now like you didn't have time for me then."

More than one thousand children from divorced families were followed from 1976 to 1987. The study showed the longer the father was out of the home, the less contact he had with his children. It goes on to say more than half of the children whose father didn't live with them had never even been to his home.[1]

As fathers, we will all reap what we sow. If we have worked on a strong, time-filled, promise-keeping relationship with our children, that relationship should still be there, even after they've grown. It's always better to work on something from the beginning, but it's never too late to start.

Weekends With Dad

Up until now, I have been speaking of fathers who choose not to spend appointed time with their children. For those of you who faithfully follow through with your scheduled time, I offer a word of caution. Over the years, I've had kids tell me two negative things about their "time with Dad."

The Couch Potato   "All we did was go over to Dad's, sit around, and watch TV." Sports on television might be stimulating to most fathers, but it really doesn't do much for kids. If all the time your children have with you is every-other weekend, plopping down in front of the tube with sports or even cartoons isn't going to be memory-building.

I realize money can be a problem. Lots of activities children want to do can be quite expensive, but there a number of them that don't cost a lot. (See Chapter Six for a list of ideas.)

Children look to their father to provide leadership in a number of areas. It's not very fun for them, if when they get to your house you say, "Well....here we are.....what shall we do...?" How about brainstorming with your children, beforehand, on things they might like to do? Then you can set up a priority list, even a tentative calendar for their times with you. People seem to operate better when things are written down. Having an event on a calendar makes it more likely you'll actually do it. With a schedule, you're better prepared, especially if you have to rent or buy equipment.

Sharing Dad   The second complaint I hear from kids about time with Dad is it isn't just time with Dad. Dad, it seems, has a girlfriend who always seems to be around. Now whatever time they have with Dad is diluted by *her*.

Children can be very anxious about sharing a parent with another person. Their initial response to that relationship may be hurt, anger and resentment. These feelings are often played out in hostility toward Dad's new friend. They may try inappropriate behavior, disrespectful speech, or physically interposing themselves between Dad and his friend. This reaction is not uncommon and needs to be heeded as a "wake-up call" for Dad: the child's needs are not being met.

A new friend, however, can be tremendously helpful if they will reach out to your child. Taking time with your child can help build a bridge of friendship. (Don't expect your child to respond overnight and without a certain amount of resistance.)

Remember, your relationship with your child needs to have a priority in your life. That's not to say there won't be time for others, but your child needs to know you haven't substituted a new relationship for the one they already have with you.

Tug-o-War

Most children love both of their parents. It is hard enough for them to cope with the break-up of their family without hearing how "bad" their mother is. Putting down your ex-wife leaves your child uncomfortably in the middle. Too often there is a desire to gain your child's understanding of the reasons why you are no longer married. Understanding is desirable, but don't let it turn into persuading your child to see only your "side of things." Because your child sees both parents, they will naturally see "both sides." Anytime they are talked into seeing only one point of view, they may feel they have betrayed the other parent. No child should be knowingly put into this position.

Beware of verbal put-downs, snide remarks, careless comments. These will not only lower you in the eyes of your child, but hurt them by hurting someone they love, namely, their mother. Never underestimate your child's ability to project reluctant feelings toward you if you directly, or indirectly, abuse their mother.

The best way to help children through the roller-coaster of divorce is for both parents to concentrate on positive comments about each other. Finding the good may not always be easy, but it harms your child to only hear the bad.

No Fault Divorce

In any separation or divorce, children often have a tendency to blame themselves. They reason, "If only I hadn't acted like that, Dad would have stayed, " or "If only I hadn't done this, Mom and Dad would still be together." They may also reason since their behavior has in someway caused the divorce, their behavior will be able to stop it. Inappropriate behavior could be their way of attempting to move the attention away from parental disputes, onto themselves.

To a child, there is no such thing as "No-Fault Divorce." If neither parent admits to participating in the

During this time, parents need to assure their children of three things:

1) *"Mom and Dad may not be feeling good about each other right now, but our differences are not your fault."*

2) *"You will be taken care of. Mom and Dad will always be there for you."*

3) *"Whichever one of us leaves the home, you will still be able to see us."*

Being Responsible

Things may not have worked out as you intended when you said, "'Til death do us part." The fact remains, you helped bring that child into the world and you are responsible for them. You are responsible for their physical, emotional, and spiritual well-being. The relationship which brought them into the world may not last, but they do.

I have known many fathers who aren't in the home, but still do a wonderful job of keeping in touch with their kids. Their children are the beneficiaries of some excellent parenting, under difficult circumstances. It works best when both parents are working in cooperation with each other to bring up their children as well as they can.

So much is said and written these days about "dead-beat dads." I hardly need to add anything to that dismal picture. There are many fathers who abandon their responsibility to their children. It is my hope, since you are reading this book, you are making a commitment to be a responsible parent to your children. I can only say, don't give up! I have seen in my own life, and in the lives of other fathers, how rewarding responsible fathering can be!

The Kid At The Window

"My dad loved me as only a father can love a son. I don't question that. But he was also a self-centered, egocentric, s.o.b who let me down when I needed him most. A part of me will always be that kid at the window, waiting and waiting with his nose pressed against the glass. Knowing that if Dad said he was coming, he was coming; but waking up curled beneath the window, alone.

"I don't want to sit and cry about the scars his actions may have left. I'd like to believe the only real damage done was to our relationship. But I have a very hard time letting people in. Trust is not an easy word for me to say, and it's almost impossible for me to feel.

"I learned a hard lesson a long time ago. It's not one I'll risk learning again.

"Now that I'm older, ironically, the tables have turned. It's Dad who seeks me out. And it's him who is let down."[2]

* * * * *

Keeping our promises. Being faithful to our children. Doing what we say we are going to do. Being responsible for, and to, those we love. That's the heart of being a father.

THE BOTTOM LINE

*Children don't need our presents,
but our presence - - a promise, kept.*

1. If you came from a divorced home, what did your father do to keep in touch?

2. What is the hardest part of being sepa rated from your children?

3. What is the most consistent thing which keeps you away from your children?

4. What are some ways you can keep in touch with your kids?

5. How are you helping your children cope with your divorce?

Chapter Eight......DAD THE MAN

When Dad's Not the Perfect Parent

"Life is an adventure in forgiveness."
Norman Cousins

The movie, "My Girl," is the story of an eleven year-old girl, named Vada. Her mother died two days after her birth. She lives with her father, who owns a mortuary. Because her mother is dead and her father is working most of the time, Vada's life is filled with a great deal of loneliness.

Into her life comes a special friend. They spend hours together at a nearby lake, fishing and talking. They ride bikes and share secrets, even a first kiss.

But this is not a story which ends "happily ever after." Vada's peers don't seem to understand her. She goes to a doctor, thinking something is wrong, but looking for someone to take an interest in her. The teacher at school she has a crush on introduces her to his fiance. Her father begins to date a woman, invading what Vada sees as her "territory." Finally, her best friend dies, of a bee sting. This dear, little girl is simply overwhelmed with emotional pain and loneliness.

I've often wondered how many Vadas there are in our world. Vadas who live out their lives lonely, feeling rejected, misunderstood by parents and peers, longing for the warmth of friendship.

At the end of "My Girl," Vada's father comes to realize how much his daughter needs him. Sitting on her bed, he talks to her about her mother's death. He reassures her it wasn't her fault. He tells her he's tried to be a good father, asking for understanding and forgiveness. The movie ends with her father giving Vada a goodnight kiss and gently pulling the covers up securely around her chin.[1]

* * * * *

Nobody's Perfect

Regardless of the ending of "My Girl," the fact remains Vada was hurt many times. For those who live out this kind of pain in real life, emotional scars can result. Life is full of injury. Parents try to shield children from as much pain as they can. They also cause their children pain.

Try as we might to do and say the right thing all of the time with our children, none of us can. We're human. We make mistakes in our life, at our job, in our family. Ironically, we may shield a child from being hurt one minute, then wound them ourselves, the next.

As fathers, we should strive to damage our children as little as possible. But zero damage, while an admirable goal, isn't realistic. We only hurt our children more, when we refuse to acknowledge the pain our inevitable mistakes cause them.

A Time to Forgive

When my son, John, was in high school, I was very proud when he got on the varsity football team. I was anxious for, not only, my son to do well but for the team to win. After John's third game of the season, I was critical of one of the boys on his team. I didn't feel his performance was contributing to their over-all success. So focused was I on this boy as player, I forgot he was also John's teammate and friend. As we talked, my son had to rebuke me.

"Dad," he reminded me, "football is just a game. You need to lighten up. He's only a junior. Besides, this is just the third game of the season!"

I spent some time thinking about what John said. I realized, I'd blown it. Later, I walked down the hall to his room. Knocking on the door, I was apprehensive, knowing I needed his forgiveness. I stepped into his room and apologized for criticizing his teammate. I asked for my son's forgiveness, which he gave.

The rest of the season was much more enjoyable to watch. I stopped thinking of football as more than it was, a game. I gave up analyzing the team, stepping down from "sideline coach" to spectator.

More than the football season becoming enjoyable, there were other benefits. For me, I knew my son would forgive me when I made a mistake. For John, he knew I'd admit when I made a mistake and asked his forgiveness.

* * * * *

If you have damaged your children is some way, you need to repair the damage. There is a way to bring healing to a broken relationship. In that practical book called Proverbs in the Bible, there is a verse (Proverbs 12:18 NIV) which says, "Reckless words pierce like a sword, but the tongue of the wise brings healing." Healing is found in one word - - *forgiveness*.

Forgiveness is the key to experience healing in relationships. Since there is no way to avoid hurting someone else, at some time in your relationship, forgiveness is the way to repair the damage. It's the spoken word bringing the two back together again. Forgiveness is the salve that makes wounds heal.

You might be tempted to say to yourself at this point, "Sure, forgiveness is easy if it's something minor! But what about forgiving someone who really hurt you?" You may be thinking about yourself and how you haven't been able to forgive your own father. You may be thinking of something you've done to your children that hurt them so much, you don't think they'll ever forgive you.

The damage may be great, but so is the power of forgiveness.

Corrie Ten Boom is the author of a book, called "The Hiding Place." It tells the real-life story of her family's efforts to hide Jews from the Nazis during World War II. Those efforts landed Corrie and her family in a concentration camp at Ravensbruck. The degradation and suffering of her years in the camp are chronicled in detail in her book. While Corrie survived the concentration camp, many of her loved ones did not. The damage Corrie endured was great.

Years after she was freed from the camp, Corrie Ten Boom returned to Germany. She came with a message of forgiveness to the German people. After her talk, a man came forward from the crowd.

"I was face-to-face," she relates, "with one of my captors and my blood seemed to freeze." The man had been one of the cruelest guards at Ravensbruck.

"A fine message, Fraulein," he told her. It was obvious he didn't know her from the thousands of women in the camp. "How good it is to know that, as you say, all our sins are at the bottom of the sea!

"You mentioned Ravensbruck in your talk. I was a guard there. But since that time, I have become a Christian. I know that God has forgiven me for the cruel things I did there, but I would like to hear it from your lips as well.

"Fraulein, will you forgive me?"

Corrie writes, "And I stood there - - I whose sins had again and again to be forgiven - - and could not forgive. Betsy (her sister) had died in that place. Could he now erase her slow and terrible death simply for the asking? It could have been many seconds that I stood there - - hand held out - - but to me it seemed hours as I wrestled with the most difficult thing I had ever had to do.

"I stood there with the coldness clutching my heart, but I know the will can function regardless of the temperature of the heart. I prayed, *Jesus, help me!* Woodenly, mechanically, I thrust out my hand into the one stretched out ot me, and I experienced an incredible thing.

"The current started in my shoulder, racing down into my arms and sprang into our clutched hands. Then this warm reconcilation seemed to flood my whole being, bringing tears to my eyes. 'I forgive you, brother,' I cried with my whole heart. For a long moment, we grasped each other's hands, the former guard, the former prisoner. I had never known the love of God so intensely as I did that moment."[2]

The damage may be great, but so is the power of forgiveness.

When Forgiveness is Hard

"Don't get mad, get even!" So the saying goes.

Forgiving another who harms us isn't a natural response. Forgiveness is something we learn to do by watching others. In turn, others watch how we forgive. From the ump in Little League who makes the bad call to the driver in the other lane who cuts us off, our response is watched by others. If we weren't shown how to forgive, if we never learned growing up, revenge can be our response when someone hurts us. We're angry. We don't want to forgive that person. It's too hard. It doesn't seem right what they did should be forgiven, they shouldn't be "let off the hook." We want to take revenge.

While revenge might feel the right thing to do, it turns out to be wrong. No less an authority than Jesus Himself tells us when someone wrongs us, we are to forgive that person. Easy to say, hard to do.

We all want others to overlook our shortcomings and forgive our mistakes. After all, we know we didn't mean anything by it, or we were just too tired, too busy, too preoccupied. We always seem to have a reason why we should be forgiven. Forgiveness isn't hard, when we're the ones who need it.

Forgiving others, though, is very difficult. Our attitude wants to be, "I've been wronged! I have my rights!" Withholding forgiveness from another may be the only power we feel we have. We may want to shove their guilt in their face over and over again, punishing them for how badly they hurt us. We want to hurt them for hurting us. But who really is hurt?

When we fail to forgive, the seeds of bitterness are planted. Like weeds growing in a garden, bitterness unchecked chokes the joy out of life. If we carry the bitterness around in our heart and mind, choosing not to forgive, cynicism and negativism will creep into our personalities.

As these personality traits take center stage, other people, innocent people, want nothing to do with us. It isn't fun being around a person who is always negative and cynical. Most people instinctively withdraw from this type of person. As people leave, loneliness arrives. Our internal seething breeds external walls and creates distance between ourselves and others.

Noted author and pastor, Bruce Larson, in his book, "There's A Lot More To Health Than Not Being Sick," relates a story of the time he visited a half-way house in Western Ontario, Canada. The residents there were emotionally disturbed. They didn't need institutional care any longer, but a place where they could relearn how to cope with life, in society.

Over the mantle of the fireplace was a beautifully framed sign. It read, "Do you want to be right or well?"[3] Sometimes becoming well means giving up the priviledge of being right.

In order for your family to be "well," it is important for you to give up the need to be "right." You may have been hurt in the past and be carrying bitterness around with you now. Even though you're right, isn't it time to be well?

Do you always need to be right with your children? Do you need to win every argument you have with them? Do you ever admit when you're wrong? Are you afraid they won't love you, if you make mistakes? Do you forgive them when they make mistakes? *Do you want to be right in your family, or do you want your family to be well?*

The Burden of Unforgiveness

When we make a choice not to forgive others, we live with a burden. Our relationship with others and self is adversely affected. We remain alienated from the one who hurt us. Our own lives become full of criticism and bitterness. We don't like ourselves and others aren't too happy with us either!

There is another relationship soured by our inability to forgive - - it is our spiritual relationship. Which of us has not heard the Lord's Prayer, especially the part that says, "And forgive us our trespasses, as we forgive those who trespass against us...?" In Matthew 6:14-15 (RSV) Jesus says, "For if you forgive men their trespasses, your Heavenly Father will forgive you; but if you do not forgive men their trespasses, neither will your Father forgive your trespasses." The critical measure we use to judge others will, in turn, judge us.

For those who worry the guilty party will somehow be "let off the hook" by God, remember the price has already been paid, for all of us, by Christ. The reason we are to forgive, then, is not to free someone from guilt. The reason we are to forgive is because withholding forgiveness is bad for us. Paul implores those who read his letter to the Ephesians to, "Let all bitterness and wrath and anger and clamor and slander be put away from you, with all malice, and be kind to one another, tenderhearted, forgiving one another as God in Christ forgave you." (Ephesians 5:23-24 RSV)

All of the important relationships in our life can be damaged by our unwillingness to forgive.

All of the important relationships in our life can be damaged by our unwillingness to *ask for forgiveness*.

Asking for Forgiveness

One of the hardest things for men to do is admit when we're wrong. It's hard to confess we've blown it. We are unwilling to put forth evidence we're not perfect. Too often that unkind word or inappropriate action is used within our own families.

Instead of trying to pretend our mistake never happened, or didn't really injure someone, we need to step forward and make it right. It's up to us to act as a catalyst for the healing process. Children don't always have the tools to "make things right" with Dad. We need to be able to choose ourselves to make things right.

For that we need an *action plan*.

FORGIVENESS ACTION PLAN

1. Take time to reflect on the situation.
2. Try to see it from the **other's point of view**.
3. **Recognize God** as the power to restore the relationship.

4. Understand our willingness to forgive makes us **agents of reconcilation**.
5. Ask God for wisdom. Ask yourself, **What would Jesus do?**
6. Consider **God's model** of forgiveness through Christ.
7. Take the initiative - - **decide to forgive.**
8. Take the initiative - - **ask for forgiveness**

How to Ask for Forgiveness

"I realize I was wrong when I _____, *and I want to ask for your forgiveness."*

"I see now how I have hurt you. I want to ask for your forgiveness."

Asking for forgiveness is more than a passing, "Sorry about that," or even a genuine, "I apologize." Asking for forgiveness is a much more humbling experience. We become vulnerable. Many of us aren't comfortable enough, or secure enough, to admit a mistake. We may view any admission of fault as a sign of weakness, rather than what it is - - a sign of strength.

For many, the pattern of forgiveness will come from our father. As we were growing up, we watched how dad handled it when he made a mistake, and when we made one. If dad wasn't the kind of man to admit a mistake or forgive anyone else's, we didn't see the healing touch of forgiveness lived out.

How can we understand and practice what we haven't seen or experienced? By going beyond our father's example to our Heavenly Father's example. Repairing relationships is nearly impossible from a human standpoint. With God's help and example of forgiving, reconciliation is possible.

Dealing With The Response

Whenever we ask for forgiveness, we can't be sure how the other person will respond. Perhaps that's why we feel so uncomfortable asking for forgiveness in the first place. There is a risk of being rejected if we ask for forgiveness. Denying we need forgiveness, however, is sure to bring about a broken relationship. One is a risk, the other is sure.

When asking for forgiveness, various responses will follow:

"Yes, I forgive you."

"I forgive you and I want to ask your forgiveness for the way I acted."

"I don't want to talk about it right now."

"No, I don't forgive you."

"No, I won't ever forgive you."

If the person forgives you, your relationship is restored. If the person doesn't want to talk about it, you'll have to wait for a later time. The person you have injured may need time to heal, to get beyond the pain before they are able to forgive. If the person refuses to forgive you, you have, at least, planted a seed to restore the relationship. Continue to pray the Lord will bring about healing. You've done what you can, for the moment.

Whichever response is given, you have taken the right step in re-establishing a relationship damaged by your actions. Your willingness to admit mistakes and ask for forgiveness provides a powerful example for your children to follow.

Loose Ends

"Why don't you get a decent job," my father said to me on many occasions. "Why don't you settle down, make some money, and stop running around with those high school kids?" He didn't approve of my call to ministry or counseling. My father didn't understand or approve of what I did with my life. He really didn't approve of who I was as an adult. That was tough to take.

Many men carry the burden of never getting approval from their father. As a result, there is a void in their heart. Something will always be missing, no matter how successful they might become. Lack of approval has left many men bitter and empty.

My emptiness came from a father who didn't approve of what I felt called to do. He reprimanded me for not having the foresight to get a well-paying job, like my brothers. While we remained friends over the years, there was still an empty place where his approval should have been. Before he died, I decided to fill up my empty place.

I started by trying to understand why my father couldn't give me approval. I don't really believe he knew how to show concern and affection. He simply didn't see life from the same perspective I did. The more I tried to persuade him, the more we seemed to argue. The very thing I needed so desperately from my father was the one thing he was unable to give. Rather than constantly be disappointed, I decided to seek out another source.

While my father couldn't give me the approval I needed, God did. Healing and forgiveness came when I realized my worth as a person wasn't found in whether or not my father approved of my profession. My worth as a person was, and is, because of my relationship with Jesus Christ.

Looking at my father through the eyes of Christ, I was able to see Dad only did what he knew to do. In so many ways, he tried to explain to me he did the best he could. I was trying so hard to win his approval, I failed to hear his apology. I don't think my father received much in the way of appreciation from his father. It shouldn't have been surprising, he didn't know how to give it.

Through Christ, I was able to forgive my father for his lack of affirmation and encouragement. When the end came for Dad, there was no unfinished business, no loose ends, in our relationship. In my heart, I could grant forgiveness to my earthly father and accept approval from my Heavenly One.

The Beauty of Forgiveness

Several years ago, a talk show host was interviewing a couple on their sixtieth wedding anniversary. Not many people today have been married that long. The host asked them to tell their secret for so many years of wedded bliss.

The old gentlemen cleared his throat and said, "Well, it comes down to one word - - forgiveness."

The host was taken aback and asked him to repeat what he'd said. Upon doing so, the host remarked, "That's very beautiful."

When forgiveness is expressed from the heart, it is very beautiful.

Vada, from the movie, "My Girl," discovered the beauty of forgiveness at the end. As her father sat on her bed, he did his best to let her know how much he cared. In his own way, he was asking for forgiveness for his shortcomings.

There are many children, young and grown, who will go to sleep tonight longing for a father who cares enough to sit at the edge of their bed. They yearn for their father to tell them how much he cares for them, to admit his mistakes and ask for their forgiveness. They want to forgive him. They want him to accept their forgiveness and tuck the covers under their chin.

If this vision can never be a reality for you and your own father, it can be with your children. They need you to help them understand the healing forgiveness can bring.

THE BOTTOM LINE

*It all comes down to one word - -
FORGIVENESS*

1. Can you recall a time when your father
    asked for your forgiveness?

2. Why do you think it is so hard to ask
    forgiveness from another person?

3. Have you ever asked for forgiveess from
    your own children?

4. What are some of the things that hold you
    back from admitting your mistakes?

Chapter Nine......DAD THE TEACHER

Teaching Respect for Authority

If we never have headaches teaching our kids
while they grow up,
we'll have plenty of heartaches after they grow up.

A study done in 1940 of the top discipline problems in school found they were: talking, gum chewing, making noise, running, dressing improperly and loitering.

A similar poll was done in 1986. The list for top discipline problems was vastly different: rape, assault, burglary, arson, bombings, murder, suicide, absenteeism, vandalism, drug abuse, alcohol abuse, gang warfare, pregnancy, abortion and venereal disease.[1]

* * * * *

From Ward Cleaver to Homer Simpson

Over the past four and a half decades, the moral and ethical fiber of our culture has literally begun to unravel. Fingers of blame are pointed at divorce to television. One of the main causes, I believe, is lack of respect for authority.

Television programming in recent years hasn't been successful showing healthy families who respect each other and authority. Shows like *The Simpsons* or *Married With Children* are very popular. The underlying premise of these shows is a dad, an adult authority figure, who is a baffoon. Whether Homer Simpson or Al Bundy, the father is portrayed as totally incompetent to handle life and family situations. The children on these shows display little respect for parents, teachers, police officers or other authority figures.

Ward Cleaver may have been stern with Beaver, but he was also a caring father and a willing teacher. The difference between right and wrong, concern for others, respect for people and their possessions were weekly lessons on *Leave It To Beaver.*

Television is a mirror on society. When the values of our culture changed, television shows changed. We went from Ward Cleaver to Homer Simpson.

Television reflects social values and, in turn, reinforces those values.

Questioning Authority

There was a time when respect for authority was strong. Crime was unacceptable and punishment swift. Today, courts seem to grant wrong-doers second, third, and fourth chances before punishment is handed down. "When the sentence for a crime is not quickly carried out, the hearts of the people are filled with schemes to do wrong," wrote the wise man, Solomon, in the book of Ecclesiastes. (Eccelesiastes 8:11 NIV)

We are living out those ancient words in our own society today. Children can now "divorce" their parents. Teachers are fearful of physical attack from students. Police officers are called derogatory names and mocked. Children kill other children and terrorize their neighborhoods. Lack of respect for authority is tearing apart our country.

Lack of respect for authority in a family can tear it apart. Parents have the responsibility to make sure children respect their authority. If the children refuse, parents have the additional responsibility of discipline. Proverbs 13:24 states, "He who loves his son, will discipline him." Discipline, done from God's perspective, is love.

Without discipline, children have no boundaries, no guidance in acceptable behavior, no one to enforce concepts of right and wrong. They are left adrift in a complicated, adult world which they have to navigate without help. The only authority they begin to accept is their own. They question anyone else's right to have authority over them. They become a law unto themselves. Over the years they turn from rebellious youth to sociopath, a person unable to connect with others.

There is a story I've heard about a nun working at a men's prison. One day in April, an inmate came up to her and asked her to buy him a Mother's Day card that he could send to his Mother. She willingly agreed, and the news traveled like wildfire. Soon, hundreds of inmates were asking her for Mother's Day cards.

Resourceful, this nun contacted a greeting card manufacturer. He obliged her request with crates of Mother's Day cards, all of which she passed out to the prisoners.

It wasn't too long after that, the nun realized Father's Day would be right around the corner. She called the card manufacturer, who responded quickly with boxes of Father's Day cards. She waited for the inmates to ask for those. None did. Years later, the nun reported she still had every one of those cards.[2]

This is not to say that every child who doesn't receive the discipline and instruction they need from a parent is going to end up in prison. What it does say, is children need their father to provide leadership in the area of discipline and proper respect.

A father who loves his children will provide discipline. A father who loves his children will show them how to respect those in authority. A father who loves his children will give the tools needed to be successful in the world.

Teaching Respect Through Discipline

"This hurts me more than it hurts you," my mother used to say, just before she paddled my behind.

Well, if it hurts you so much to spank me, why do you do it? As a child, I never did have the nerve to ask her that question. As an adult, I didn't need to. She wanted the best for me, which included helping me to understand right from wrong. The hard way was sometimes the only way to get through to me, as a child.

She spanked me several times growing up. I've joked over the years that my ample posterior, an Olsen trait, was really a result of those years of discipline. "My mother was a strong disciplinarian," I'd say. "The swelling *still* hasn't gone down!"

As much as I joke, I love my mother for loving me enough to discipline. It wasn't easy for her. And it hasn't been easy for me with my own children. But I believe what the Scriptures say about the positive effect of discipline:

"My son, do not make light of the Lord's discipline, and do not lose heart when he rebukes you; because the Lord disciplines those he loves, and he punishes everyone he accepts as a son.

"Endure hardship as discipline. For what son is not disciplined by his father? If you are not disciplined (and everyone undergoes discipline), then you are illegitimate children and not true sons.

"Moreover, we all have had human fathers who disciplined us and we respected them for it. How much more should we submit to the Father of our spirits and live!

"Our fathers disciplined us for a little while as they thought best; but God disciplines us for our good, that we may share in his holiness.

"No discipline seems pleasant at the time, but painful. Later on, however, it produces a harvest of righteousness and peace for those who have been trained by it." (Hebrews 12:5-11 NIV)

Discipline produces respect and trains a child for life.

What To Do When Your Rules Are Broken

1. Let your kids know who is in charge (you!).
2. Set specific rules and consequences for breaking the rules.
3. Be consistent enforcing the rules.
4. Let your kids know the rules are there because you love them.

Rule #1: Let your kids know who is in charge.

From the beginning, children need to know who is in charge. If there is a power void (i.e. the one in charge isn't well defined), children will automatically seek to fill that void. Being vague or nonspecific about the leadership role in the family provides children a loophole large enough to charge through!

All children will test the boundaries, just to make sure you still mean them. Don't be surprised when this happens. They're making sure the world, as they know it, still exists. When they test the boundaries, and the boundaries hold, their world is secure.

As your children play with other children, house rules will probably be compared. Your son may come home wondering why Timmy gets to stay up until midnight watching Triple Horror Feature and he doesn't. Remember to emphasize, you're in charge of your family. And each family will have their own rules.

Rule #2: Set specific rules and consequences for breaking those rules.

Set your rules before situations arise where your children test you. Having your rules and consequences established before you have to use them keeps you from reacting in the anger and frustration of the moment. You won't have to come up with spur-of-the-moment, heat-of-the-moment, solutions.

As your children get older, try having a family council. Together, go over how the rules are changing as their responsibilities grow. Have your children recommend consequences if they don't keep the rules. By participating in the rules and consequences, they will be more apt to abide by the rules. When the consequences come, they won't seem so "unfair" if your children have had a say in what they are.

A word of caution: Try to have as few rules as possible. You can encompass a great many situations with a rule like, "Show respect for people and their possessions." That rule will cover Sister borrowing Brother's mitt, to riding bikes over Mrs. Gardner's petunias, to speaking nicely to each other in conversation.

Rule #3: Be consistent enforcing the rules.

Rules are useless unless enforced. Unenforced rules are merely suggestions. If you don't enforce your rules, they will be taken as just suggestions.

This is probably the hardest part of disciplining. We all have good intentions of "standing firm" in our resolve to uphold the rules. But then the moment-of-truth comes, with big, teary eyes and a mouthful of earnest excuses. Or we are confronted with a steely stare and clenched jaw. Either innocence personified or defiance extraordinare - - that's when it becomes difficult to discipline.

The will of a child far outweighs whatever the scale says. Two year-olds can exhibit the will of a lion when confronted. They want to win.

You need to win. If you fail to enforce your own rules, you and the rules will not be respected. More and more situations will turn into battlefields. Holding firm in one area can save you confrontation in another. Stand firm.

Rule #4: Let your kids know the rules are there because you love them.

"No discipline seems pleasant at the time, but painful. Later on, however, it produces a harvest of righteousness and peace for those who have been trained by it." (Hebrews 12:11 NIV)

Love and concern for their welfare should be the motivation for your rules and discipline. Anger and revenge for wrong-doing have no place in disciplining children. Rules aren't to "get even" with a disobedient child .

The overriding lesson your children should learn from your discipline is, you love them. It can start as young as telling a toddler not to go into the street so they aren't hit by a car. If they disobey, you must discipline them. Not because you want to, but because you care, most of all, for their safety.

The Need for Discipline

When my children were young, they displayed their self-centered natures early. If John and I were playing a game, John would always want to be first up. With an indoor boardgame, John would always announce, "Me first!" and proceed to roll the dice or spin the spinner. With an outdoor game, he wanted to be the first to bat or receive the kick-off.

Megen decided which toys her friends could play with. If one of her playmates reached for a different toy, Megen would try to snatch it away from the startled child, yelling, "Mine! Mine!" If that didn't work, she would usually start crying as the two battled over the toy.

As their father, I didn't teach them this behavior. I didn't say to John, "Now, son, whenever you get into a game, exclaim 'Me first!' and jump in before any one else has a chance." Nor did I teach Megen, "Honey, whenever you want a toy someone else is playing with, scream loudly, 'Mine! Mine!' and grab that toy with all your might! If screaming doesn't work, Megen, try crying at the top of your lungs."

We are, by nature, self-seeking. Children seek to define the rules they live by. They resist attempts to conform to someone else's set of rules. Discipline helps train them to accept another's authority.

As fathers, we must teach children right from wrong, respect for others and those in authority. If we don't teach them right from wrong, they won't know the difference and will injure themselves by wrong choices. If we don't teach them respect for others they won't grow to respect themselves. If they never learn to respect authority, they will have a hard time in life getting along with peers, teachers, employers, police, anyone else in established authority. In short, they will have a hard time with life.

Spare The Rod - Spoil The Child

I know I will lose some of you here, as I talk about physical correction. The "rod" sounds so punishing. While it is hard to think of using physical force to discipline a child, there is ample evidence this is an acceptable means of obtaining compliance.

"He who spares the rod hates his son, but he who loves him is careful to discipline him." (Proverbs 13:24 NIV)

"Discipline your son, for in that there is hope." (Proverbs 19:18 NIV)

"Folly is bound up in the heart of a child, but the rod of discipline drives it far from him." (Proverbs 22:15 NIV)

"The rod of correction imparts wisdom, but a child left to himself disgraces his mother." (Proverbs 29:15 NIV)

"Discipline your son, and he will give you peace; he will bring delight to your soul." (Proverbs 29:17 NIV)

"Do not withhold discipline from a child; if you punish him with a rod he will not die. Punish him with a rod and save his soul from death." (Proverbs 23:13 NIV)

While using your hand or small paddle on the buttocks is acceptable, hitting a child in anger never is. Hitting across the face with an open hand is not correction, it is physical abuse. You must be in control and confident of your reasons when you are forced to discipline. Be able to say, like my mother, "This is going to hurt me more than it hurts you."

For a more detailed study on disciplining your children, it would be of great value for you to read the book, "Dare to Discipline" by Dr. James Dobson. He provides an in-depth, practical look at disciplining children.

A Word of Caution

Just as the Scriptures give an imperative to take disciplining seriously, it also sounds a word of warning. "Fathers, do not exasperate your children; instead, bring them up in the training and instruction of the Lord." (Ephesians 6:4 NIV)

The writer, Paul, is encouraging fathers to guard against discouraging a child by excessive criticism or harsh discipline. He feels so strongly in this area, he goes on to say in another book, "Fathers, do not embitter your children, or they will become discouraged." (Colossians 3:21 NIV)

Be wise in how you discipline your children. Done improperly, they can end up embittered and discouraged. Done well, you can help train them to function as happy, well-adjusted adults.

How To Raise A Delinquent

The Houston, Texas, Police Department produced an insightful list of rules for raising delinquent children. While humorous in one way, they are also heart-breaking in another.

1. Begin in infancy to give your child everything she wants. This way she will grow up believing society owes her a living.

2. When he picks up vulgar words, laugh at him. This will make him think he's cute.

3. Never give her spiritual training. Wait until she's 21 and let her decide for herself.

4. Always avoid using the word, "wrong." He may develop a guilt complex. This will condition him later when he's arrested that society is against him and he's being persecuted.

5. Pick up everything she leaves lying around the house. Do everything for her so she will be experienced at placing all responsibility on others.

118

6. Let him read any printed matter he gets his hands on. Be careful to make sure what he touches is clean, but never mind what he reads is filthy.

7. Quarrel frequently in front of your children. This way they won't be shocked when the family breaks up.

8. Give the child all the spending money she wants. Never make her earn her own.

9. Satisfy his every craving for food, drink and comfort. See that every sensual desire is gratified. Hold nothing back.

10. Take her part against neighbors, officers of the law and teachers. They're all prejudiced against your child.

11. When he gets into trouble, apologize for yourself and say, "I could never do anything with that boy, anyway."

12. Prepare yourself for a life full of grief.[3]

A Thick Milkshake vs. Soggy Potato Chips

My mother often took my brother, Tom, and I shopping in downtown Seattle, Washington on Saturdays. This wasn't my favorite week-end activity. However, for being "good boys," our reward was a thick chocolate milkshake and egg salad or tuna sandwich at noon. It was worth it to me to behave myself shopping, so I could have that wonderful shake for lunch! Mom didn't have to scold us over and over during the morning to behave. We knew if we didn't, no milkshake.

When we did behave and receive our reward, my brother and I felt ten-feet tall.

"When you see a child behave well," says noted children's authority, Dr. Fitzhugh Dodson, "reward him with praise. A smile, a hug, or a pat on the shoulder. Do something that indicates you think he is a special person."[4]

MY FATHER, MY HERO

It is interesting to note, sometimes, children get more attention by misbehaving than by behaving. When this happens, children will make it a habit to misbehave, to see how much attention they can get.

Dr. Dodson calls this, "The Law of the Soggy Potato Chip." It goes like this: "A child naturally prefers a fresh, crisp potato chip to a soggy one. But if the only chip the child can get is soggy, he'll take it. In other words, a child ordinarily wants positive attention from his parents, but if the only attention he can get is negative, he'll settle for that. It's better than none at all."[5]

I probably would have settled for soggy potato chips from my mother. I'm glad I behaved and she gave me a milkshake, instead.

Encouraging Acceptable Behavior

Here are several ways you can encourage acceptable behavior in your children.

WAYS TO ENCOURAGE ACCEPTABLE BEHAVIOR

1. Talk with your child as you would with a friend. Don't always use a command, give a direction or say a negative comment.

2. Be honest with your child. Build trust by keeping your promises.

3. Take a trip to the police or fire station. Build up authority figures. Speak highly of teacher and leaders.

4. "Contract" with your children for rewards for certain behaviors.

5. Be consistent with both discipline and rewards.

6. Put yourself in your child's position. When you respond with empathy, your child feels you are on their side.

7. Communicate with "I messages" instead of "You messages." For example, "I feel frustrated when you track mud in the house," instead of "You never watch where you're going! Look at the mess you made!"

Teach The Magic Word

Teaching respect for authority begins early, with simple manners. When John and Megen were small, we had magic words used when they wanted something.

"Can I have that, Dad?" one of them would ask.

"What's the magic word," I'd say.

"Pleeeeaaaasssseee," they'd respond, drawing out the syllable. If I could, I'd give them what they asked for.

Simple manners of "please" and "thank you" teach children common courtesy. They learn how to get along with other people.

Teach your children how to meet new people. Show them how to shake someone's hand. Remind them to say, "It was nice to meet you," when they leave. Meeting new people can be awkward. Having a strategy helps ease the tension.

Instead of just saying, "Hi," for a greeting, encourage your children to learn names. "I'm happy to meet you, Mr. Smith," or "Nice to meet you, Mrs. Jones," sound better than a softly mumbled, generic greeting. Names are important, a prized possession for each person. Using another person's name shows respect.

Teach your children the little courtesies in life that go a long way: standing up when a woman enters the room, opening the door for another person, allowing someone else to go ahead in line, giving up a seat, helping an elderly person. These small actions build a foundation for respecting others.

Table manners are so often neglected these days. Seems everyone is rushing just to get through dinner. Table manners need to be stressed: wait to eat until all members are seated, ask for things to be passed instead of reaching across the table, asking to be excused from the table when finished, taking their own plate to the kitchen.

These little acts, of magic words and simple deeds, teach big lessons to our children and set the stage for successful interactions as adults. Teaching these little acts is the least we can do.

Children who respect and honor their parents are children who understand, through careful training, what it means to respect others and themselves. Take the lead in teaching your children this valuable lesson.

THE BOTTOM LINE

*Endure the headaches of discipline now,
and save the heartaches later.*

1. In what ways did your father help you respect authority?

2. Why do you think respect for authority in this country is declining?

3. What lesson is your own behavior towards authority teaching your children?

4. Re-read "What To Do When Your Rules Are Broken" (page 128). Which step do you need to work on the most?

Chapter Ten......DAD THE PEACEMAKER

How To Handle Conflicts

My children, like most others, occasionally had disagreements with each other. There were older-younger conflicts and boy-girl conflicts. One Saturday morning, as I was in the kitchen cleaning up from breakfast, a conflict broke out between them over a pad of writing paper. I guess they were just bored of watching cartoons that morning. All of a sudden, shouts could be heard from the other room.

Tired of their bickering, I yelled out, "That's it! Both of you, go to your rooms and think about it!"

Pulling Rank + Giving Orders = Peace and Quiet.

All right, nothing was solved, but it sure was calm in the house. A few minutes later, I realized I wasn't accomplishing anything by avoiding the problem. Now, along with being mad at each other, they were also mad at me!

Going to each of their rooms, I invited them out into the living room. "I'd like you to help me with something," I told them. Intrigued enough to stop sulking, they shuffled into the living room.

"I'd like to try my problem-solving skills on you," I said. "I'd like to see how well they work, okay?"

The response wasn't what I'd call enthusiastic, but they agreed to my little experiment.

"First of all," I started, "what do each of you see as the problem here?"

Megen immediately jumped in. "I want to draw on the writing tablet!"

John, not to be outdone, rushed forward with, "It was my idea first! Besides, I'm older. I should be able to use it before Megen!"

Problem identified: two children, one writing tablet.

"What do you think we should do about this problem?" I asked next. We talked over possible solutions, everything from time limits on the pad to putting it away altogether. (No one seemed to like that idea.) John and Megen took turns evaluating each solution. They gave their opinions as to why each solution would, or wouldn't, work for them.

As we talked it out, I knew I'd have to make the final decision. Solomon-like, I suggested a solution.

"This writing tablet has a gummed top," I said, showing them the shiny, rubberized strip along the top of the pad. "I'll tear the tablet in half and each of you will get one."

John and Megen agreed to my solution, as long as the two halves were as even as humanly possible. We talked about the solution and how we arrived at it. They went happily on their way, each with a tablet in hand.

As I went back to the kitchen, I thought to myself, it hadn't taken that much time to work out a solution. It certainly was better than yelling, "Go to your rooms!" Instead of taking the easy way out, I invested a little of my time and effort to teach my children how to resolve a disagreement.

* * * * *

As individuals, all of us have our own unique personality, temperament, characteristics, idiosyncrasies. When these are not in synch with others, disagreements, arguments, even fights occur. We need to teach our children ways of dealing with these inevitable conflicts.

I'm not speaking here of earth-shattering conflicts. (Those will be discussed in Chapter Twelve when I deal with teenagers!) For small children, conflicts arise when two want the same toy, the last piece of cake, the front seat of the car, or the new puppy to sleep with. Insignificant to us, they are important and remembered by children.

I'll never forget one pick-up game of baseball I had as a child. A group of the neighborhood kids got together one afternoon. It was a great game. The pitchers were throwing slow so even the smaller kids could get a hit. The teams were divided up evenly and everyone got to play. Close calls were decided by majority vote. It was wonderful!

One of the players on the team opposing mine was called out on a close call at first base. He wasn't thrilled with "majority rules" and started yelling at the top of his lungs. It wasn't long before his teammates joined him. Soon, we were all yelling, shouting and screaming, as only frustrated children can. The boy who was called out reached down and, picking up the bat and ball which happened to be his, went home. End of game!

It's been over forty years since that afternoon. I still see that "boy" every once in a while. "I was safe," he'll joke to me.

"You were out," I'm still quick to respond.

We can chuckle about it now, but back then, it was a big deal. It ruined our game and it took time for all of us to enjoy playing together.

Conflict Resolution of Biblical Proportions

None of us is perfect. We make mistakes. We get irritated with each other. Recognizing some sort of conflict is inevitable, we need to teach our children appropriate ways of dealing with it.

PEACEMAKING PRINCIPLES

1. Take your conflict to the Lord first.

2. Talk to the other person in private

3. Allow a third party to mediate.

4. Continue to give the situation to the Lord.

"If your brother sins against you, go and show him his fault, just between the two of you. If he listens to you, you have won your brother over. But if he will not listen, take one or two others along, so that every matter may be witnessed by the testimony of two or three witnesses." (Matthew 18:15-16 NIV)

1. Take your conflict to the Lord first.

All aspects of our relationships, including the disagreements, are important to God. Before responding in a conflict, take the situation to the Lord first. Ask Him to give you His perspective on what happened. Ask for His wisdom in how to reconcile with the other person. Take time to pray for the other person and ask God to prepare the way for reconciliation.

Sometimes we don't ever confront the one we're in conflict with. After all, we've just had a disagreement with them! Avoiding them, and the problem, seems easier than confronting. There's always a risk as to how they will respond. Pray and trust God to be with you when you go to the other person.

2. Talk to the other person in private.

The more serious the disagreement, the better it will be to meet face-to-face. Try asking the other person out for a cup of coffee or lunch. If that's not possible, a phone call will have to do.

The words you use, and the spirit in which they are spoken, will set the tone for your meeting. If your words come across as judgmental or accusatory, the other person may put up a defensive wall. The door will effectively close for productive discussion and reconcilation.

With my children, I tried to stick with the phrase, "I need some help in understanding why this happened." Using this method, several important steps are accomplished. One, it focuses on you and your feelings, not on them and their actions. By removing the accusation and sticking with how it made you feel, arguments are less likely to happen.

Remember, each person has their own view of events. If you try to focus on the event itself, you will probably have two views. When dealing with feelings, only you can explain how the event made you feel. It's harder to argue with feelings. Secondly, using this method will open up the other person to explain their side of things, in a non-hostile environment.

3. Allow a third party to mediate.

If your disagreement is the kind that needs to be resolved, but you're unable to achieve resolution on your own, try bringing in a third party. Businesses across this country, from labor unions to baseball owners, use mediators to help resolve difficult issues. A mediator is generally a trustworthy third party, who has nothing personal to gain from favoring one side over the other in a conflict.

In my counseling, I am often put in the role of mediator. People will come to me, either with the other person or alone, seeking my advice on how to handle a particular problem. They are looking for someone else to bring a fresh approach to an old problem.

I recently heard of some students being used as mediators in their grade school. Their job is to break up arguments and fights during recesses and lunch. Trained in conflict resolution skills, these students are having success in cutting down the number of problems arising from school yard conflicts.

Several years ago, a friend of mine told me he regularly saw two young boys arguing with each other on their way to and from school. They would pass daily in front of his house and he was afraid they'd eventually come to blows. He asked my advice on what to do if they did. I suggested a simple approach.

Sure enough, it wasn't long after,. the boys started fighting right in front of his house. Instead of yelling at them to "take it somewhere else!" he stepped out onto the sidewalk and asked their names.

Talking to them in a friendly manner, he asked each what the problem was. As they began to explain their side, he was able to suggest solutions. After a few minutes, the boys decided on one. They shook hands and walked the rest of the way home together.

An interested third party invested a few minutes of his time and energy to teach them how to get along. He provided them with another point view.

4. Continue to give the situation to the Lord.

Not everyone is going to respond to this method. They may not appreciate your efforts at reconciliation.

In fact, you may catch a full blast of wrath for even trying. The key to maintaining hope for a positive resolution is how you choose to respond.

When you feel yourself being verbally attacked, instead of retaliating, try saying, "I didn't realize you felt that way." In doing so, you accomplish two things. First, by letting them vent their anger, to "blow off steam", they may eventually come to the point they can discuss the situation rationally. Secondly, it reassures them you are really listening to their side of the story.

Occasionally, you run into a person who refuses to be reconciled to you. You've tried everything you can think of to make it right, but still they don't respond. In that case, you can find inner peace in knowing you did what you could.

Continue to pray about that person and the situation. Remember, God cares about your relationships. "Therefore, if you are offering your gift at the altar and there remember that your brother has something against you, leave your gift there in front of the altar. First go and be reconciled to your brother; then come and offer your gift." (Matthew 5:23-24 NIV)

Keep trying and keep praying! Resolving conflict takes time. In our fast paced, do-it-now, world, we don't often take the time to sit down and talk or reflect. We especially don't find time in our busy schedules to talk over an argument. It's unpleasant to deal with and we can find a hundred and one other things to do. Denying the problem exists doesn't make it go away.

Problem-Solving Suggestions

When your kids argue and fight, teach them to use the following method. Take time, yourself, to use their disagreements as "teaching moments" when you can impress upon them the need to work out their problems.

1. Define the Problem. Give each person the opportunity to present the problem, as they see it. Others must listen and not interrupt.

2. List Possible Solutions. Give each person the opportunity to give input. This is the brainstorming segment. There are no right or wrong answers and no evaluations.

3. Evaluate Each Solution. Now is the time to go over each solution presented and evaluate its effectiveness. Each person's input is respected.

4. Select One Solution. Allow each person to choose one solution from those agreed upon.

5. Set a Time Limit. Agree to try the selected solution for a specific period of time, such as a day, week or "until next month."

6. Re-evaluate the Selected Solution. At the end of the time limit, get each person back together and evaluate how well the solution is working. If it is not, go back to step four and try another solution or go back to step one and start over.

This conflict resolution process is fairly simple. It can be used with your children, spouse, co-workers, on committees, and generally in all situations where people are willing to come together to talk out their differences.

Blessed Are the Peacemakers

Your children need you to model peacemaking. Without you, they may not have opportunity to see it any place else. The thousands of hours of violence they see on televsion won't prepare them to be peacemakers. From television all they learn about conflicts is they end in an hour at the end of a gun. From classmates they may learn inappropriate ways of dealing with conflict. No, Dad, it's up to you.

Remember to keep your words and actions in agreement as well! Do you counsel your daughter on how to get along with her best friend and then yell at her for a minor inconvenience? Do you spend time talking to your son about how to understand a difficult classmate only to honk your horn and yell at another driver? Your children will measure your words by your actions. Make sure both are in agreement.

My mother used to say, "You catch more flies with honey than you do with vinegar." Teach your children to use honey-coated words and actions when dealing with others. Show them how to live at peace.

Your children will never live in a conflict-free environment. Disagreements are, and will be, a part of their daily lives. Model successful conflict resolution in your own life and teach those skills to your children.

THE BOTTOM LINE

*Seek to live in peace with all
and teach your children to do the same.*

1. When you were in grade school, do you remember a time when you had an argument or confrontation?

2. How were you raised to deal with conflicts?

3. How do you resolve conflicts today?

4. What lessons about conflict resolution are you passing on to your children.

5. Looking at your children, how does each handle disagreements with others?

Chapter Eleven......DAD THE HEALER

Guiding Your Child
Through Difficult Times

Butterflies are marvelous collages of color. We see them in flight, with the sun shining off of their spectacular wings, forgetting sometimes what it takes to make butterflies beautiful. We see the beautiful butterfly and forget the hairy, crawling caterpillar.

Butterflies start out as eggs, laid in plant leaves which later become their food. The eggs hatch into wormlike larvae. These larvae grow into the caterpillars we see making their way up trees or across sidewalks. Earthbound, we hardly pay them any attention.

After several weeks of eating those plant leaves, caterpillars enter a third stage of life, called a pupa or resting state. They begin to make cocoons around themselves where they will stay for a few weeks or all winter. It is during this resting stage the hairly, crawling caterpillar turns into a butterfly or moth. This transformation is call metamorphosis.

When the resting stage is complete, the butterfly struggles to get out of the cocoon through a tiny opening. This struggling, at first, may seem cruel but it's God's way of forcing fluid into the the butterfly's wings so it can fly. The struggle to grow and change helps the butterfly to soar.

So it is with our children.

* * * * *

As painful as it is to watch our children struggle through difficulty, as easy as it would be to just "fix it" for them, they need the experience so they, too, will be able to "fly." The trick for us, as parents, is to know when to step in and when to back off. This delicate balance is reflected in the following poem by Ann McMurray:

Cliff of Life

And when my child had come of age,
When he would face the world, outside,
I tied around the Rope of Trust.
He gently down the slope did slide.

At first, the angle of descent,
Was easy, in its gradual way.
But Cliff of Life, it lay beyond.
My heart was fearful for that day.

My child's voice did then arise,
And asked for me to give more slack.
He thought I held the Rope too tight.
"Besides," he said, "I've got the knack!"
I thought it over carefully,
Then gave the Rope to slip, at last.
Several coils lept through my hands,
Before I saw it went too fast.

A grip of panic clutched my throat.
My hands, they latched upon the Rope.
The hemp burned furrows in my palm.
I searched inside for inner calm.

My voice, it filtered down the Cliff.
I craned my head in hopes to see.
No sound arose beyond the depths.
Oh where, oh where could my child be?

"Father, Father," he cried, at last.
"Be relieved, for I'm alright.
I just went down a bit too fast.
I only got a bump and fright."

The wave of panic washed away,
Receeding down from whence it came.
Then anger quickly took its place.
My hands would never be the same!

"Father, Father," my child did shout.
"Please tell me why you are so slow?
For you have tightened on the Rope,
And there is nowhere I can go!"

Then, the truth, it came to me,
This was called the Rope of TRUST.
For him to ever travel on,
The giving out of slack - - a must!

I gently eased up on the Rope,
But now, the slack is such a sort,
That should, again, the Rope stream past,
It will slow, with my support.

Children have to experience life on their own. It is our job, as parents and fathers, to support them throught those experiences. We can be there during the triumphant times, to laugh and shout for joy. We must be there during the difficult times, when things don't turn out as expected.

Winning and Losing

One of the hardest lesson, for anyone, is how to accept a setback. The first line of defense is often to blame others for the disappoint or failure. Defeat is hard to live with, especially when we've caused it to happen.

"We're Number One! We're Number One!" I can't tell you how many times I heard that chant, screamed at football, basketball or baseball games. Index finger jabbed proudly in the air. Nothing but Number One was good enough.

We live in a success-oriented culture. Whatever we do, whatever we buy, must be the very best. Advertising tells us by buying the very best, we are, too. The message is: "Buy Number One - - Be Number One!"

The hard fact of life is, we can't all be number one. Very few will actually achieve that distinction. I can remember two times in my life when I was judged Number One. The first had nothing to do with me. I was the first born in my family. I've always been Son Number One. The second Number One I can remember is from fifth grade. I won a spelling contest that year. I know, not exactly a red-letter event, but it was a pretty big deal for me at the time. I'll never forget how I felt, being Number One over every one else.

Winning in life is a wonderful thing. It's great to rejoice with our children when they win a game or a contest. We try to help them win with grace and style, with sportsmanship. It feels good when they win.

But life isn't about winning. Most of the time, we don't. Life is really about learning how to deal with losses and second and last places. We want our children to find some stability in the midst of their disappointments. We need to teach them being "Number One" isn't all there is in life. If we don't, they'll end up disillusioned when they are unable to win all of the time.

By teaching our children how to handle loss, we can set a pattern for turning failure into a learning experience. It has been said, "We learn more by our failures than our successes." Every failure teaches you something which should enable you to try again, incorporating what you've learned. As a child, were you ever told, "If at first you don't succeed, try and try again." The implication was everytime you failed, you learned something to help you succeed the next time.

Nothing Special

Most of us realize we're generally pretty average in most things. But each of us possesses something unique and special, something nobody else has. We may not be Number One all of the time, but that doesn't mean we have to feel like we're "nothing special." Each one of us is special and somehow, through the midst of peer pressure and media pressure, we need to make sure we communicate "specialness" to our children.

As our children struggle, like the butterfly, to emerge with their own unique identity, we need to encourage them to explore and experience their special nature. The fact they don't win all of the time at sports or school or relationships shouldn't cause them to conclude they're "nothing special." In order to counteract this impression, we need to shower our children with love, affirmation and affection. If we don't, they will experience stunted personal growth.

Listen to the feelings of an "average" child.

I don't cause teachers trouble. My grades have been okay.
I listen in my classes. I'm in school every day.
My teachers think I'm average. My parents think so, too.
I wish I didn't know that 'cause there's lots I'd like to do.

I'd like to build a rocket with a book that tells me how.
Or start a stamp collection. Well, no use trying now.
'Cause since I found I'm average, I'm just smart
      enough to see,
And know there's nothing special I should expect from
      me.

I'm part of the majority, that "hump" part of the bell.
Who spends his life unnoticed in an "average" sort of
      hell.[1]

The thoughts reflected in this poem mirror what I've heard from many students. They have little sense of self-worth, muddling through each day. With the right kind of encouragement, a child can understand life is made up of more than just "winners and losers." In the middle is a large group of people who do both on a regular basis. Winning, while enjoyed, isn't expected and losing, while expected, can be learned from.

Being There

One afternoon, my daughter, Megen, met me at the front door when I got home from work. There weren't any squeals of delight at seeing me. The emotion she displayed was relief.

In tears, she told me our dog, Taffy, had died. She was a ten year-old cocker spaniel, and hadn't been in the best of health. We all knew her time was coming, but nothing prepared us for the shock of her death. Megen was the one who found her, lying dead, on the back porch.

Crying, she told me how she'd found Taffy and gently laid a blanket over her limp body. I immediately sat down with her, held her tight, and cried with her. She was a great dog, loved by all of us. We recounted together the fun times Taffy had provided. We talked about how it felt to lose a friend. We just needed to hold each other, cry together.

*   *   *   *   *

A child who has experienced a disappointment of some sort needs understanding and support. They don't need a lot of advise, a list of "should-have-done's." Sometimes, they don't need to talk at all, just for you to be there for them with a listening ear.

Everyone has their own share of problems, disappointments, heartaches, pain, failures and unrealized expectations. There is a time for us as fathers to step forward and help rectify a situation. There is also a time to help the child handle the difficulty with good instruction. Finally, there is the time we must allow the child to work through the struggle themselves. But how do you know which time the current situation is?

Step One - - Listen

When a child encounters a difficulty, and comes to you, take time to listen to your child. Often because of time constraints, you may be tempted to just tell them what to do. Dads are like that: fix it and get on with life.

When John was playing football, I kept trying to "fix" his performance.

Somewhere along the line, I decided I should take time to just listen to how he was feeling about the game, instead of just barging ahead with my unsolicited advice. Now, whether John's team won or lost, we'd take several minutes after the game to talk about it. I attempted to keep my comments on the positive side. John would talk about the good things he thought he and the team had done. I'd try to bring up specific things he did right like defending his man in basketball or throwing to second base to nail the runner or opening up a hole in the offensive line for his runner to go through.

Only after emphasizing the positive did we discuss the things he could have done differently. "Perhaps you could have done this," I'd say, still keeping my words encouraging. John always seemed to have his own suggestions, too.

Our time after the game went from my critical analysis to a joint celebration of all the things done right and an exploration in how to improve. The key to our conversations, though, was my listening to John and allowing him to come to his own conclusions about the game.

With younger children, listening and finding out what is bothering them can be tough. They may take a while to get around to what's really bothering them. It may have nothing to do with the cat scaring them by running through the room. The reason they're really crying is because the neighbor next door yelled at them for running through his flower beds.

Whatever the age of the child, and however long it takes to get to the heart of the matter, keep at it. If you provide a listening, sympathetic ear for the three year-old, the fifteen year-old will know where to go.

By listening, you have a better chance of deciding yourself how much advice to give, how much intervening to do, how much slack to give your child to solve their own problem.

Learning Through Adversity

One thing was very evident with John and I as we'd talk through his games. We learned alot more about the game, about ourselves, when the team lost. Obviously, the idea in sports is to win, but when John won, we weren't nearly as careful in our game analysis as when he lost. Sometimes, after a win, our talks would be very brief. Losing and dealing with adversity brought us closer together.

"Builds character, Dad," John would say when he lost. He meant it as a humorous remark to help himself get over the loss, but he was right.

How we handle success is important, but more important can be the way we work through the hard times, frustrations and disappointments in life. Do we pout and blame others for our mistakes?

"My team didn't play like they should! I was the only one holding up the team!"

"The boss is a jerk! He's got no reason to complain about my work!"

"If only the end hadn't dropped the ball in the fourth quarter."

Teach your children to admit their mistakes and look for ways to do things differently in the future. Help them to understand sometimes they'll do everything right, and it still won't be enough. Help them to believe even though they don't see an immediate, positive result from their actions, they may yet by being patient.

By far the greatest asset I've had in helping my children deal with life's adversity is by sharing with them my faith. I truly believe Romans 8:28, which says, "Everything that happens fits into a pattern for good." (Phillips translation) Even if, at the moment, I didn't see the good, I've tried to have faith it would come. Life is hard and God is good!

Sharing my faith with my children, showing them that God is a vital part of my every day life, has made it easier to pass on this perspective. God has been with me through many difficult times. Because of that, I've had faith He will continue to be with me. I have tried to teach my children, "I don't know what the future holds, but I know Who holds the future." If you are having trouble helping your children see beyond the difficulty of the day and into the promise of the future, I recommend finding encouragement from the Scriptures.

An Encouraging Word

Times of discouragement, disillusion and despair are not far from any of us. The Scriptures can bring us encouragement, comfort and inner peace. These are what we should share with our children.

"For I know the plans I have for you, says the Lord, plans for welfare and not for evil, to give you a future and a hope." (Jeremiah 29:11 RSV)

"....even these may forget, yet I will never forget you. Behold, I have graven you on the palms of my hand." (Isaiah 49:15, 16 RSV)

"This I know, that God is for me." (Psalm 56:9 RSV)

"As I was with Moses, so I will be with you; I will not fail you or forsake you." (Joshua 1:5 RSV)

"Blessed is the man who trusts in the Lord, whose trust is in the Lord. He is like a tree planted by water, that sends out its roots by the stream, and does not fear when the heat comes, for its leaves remain green, and is not anxious in the year of the drought, for it does not cease to bear fruit." (Jeremiah 17:7-8 RSV)

"I am with you always, to the close of the age." (Matthew 28:20 RSV)

"Cast all your anxieties on Him, for He cares about you." (I Peter 5:7 RSV)

And, of course, Psalm 23:

The Lord is my shepherd, I shall not be in want. He makes me lie down in green pastures, he leads me beside the quiet waters, he restores my soul. He guides me in paths of righteousness for his name's sake. Even though I walk through the valley of the shadow of death, I will fear no evil, for you are with me; your rod and your staff, they comfort me. You prepare a table before me in the presence of my enemies. You anoint my head with oil; my cup overflows. Surely goodness and love will follow me all the days of my life, and I will dwell in the house of the Lord forever.

Share these words with your children. Share your faith in God and your confidence in the future with them, as well.

Why Me, God?

At some point, you or your children will ask this question. Something will happen which is painful and makes no sense. In the pain and anguish of the moment, it is important to communicate trust in God. After all, if we knew all the answers we'd be God, ourselves. It is left to us to trust that He loves us, knows what is best for us, and will guide us into understanding at a later time.

Like the flame of a candle in the deepening night, so God's love burns brighter in the dark hours. In that lightless, barren night, when we get blind-sided by injury to body or soul, what do we tell our children when they ask, "How come this happened to me, Dad?"

You may not be able to come up with an answer. Your only response may be to hold your child, cry with them, listen as they pour out their feelings to you.

As much as you may want, you cannot shield your child from life's pain. You can, however, walk with them through the painful situations of their lives, loving them, supporting them, encouraging them, believing in their ability to learn and go on. By doing so, you'll help them to heal. Sometimes, that's the most you can do.

THE BOTTOM LINE

*Help your children to learn
from their struggles to fly free.*

1. Can you remember as a child feeling especially disappointed or hurt by an event that did, or didn't, happen?

2. How did your father respond to you during this time?

3. What struggles are your children going through now, in their life?

4. How can you respond today to those struggles and help your child learn from them?

Chapter Twelve......DAD THE SURVIVOR

Help! There's A Teenager In The House!

When my son, John, was in high school, we decided one night to go see a movie. Megen was staying at a friend's house overnight, so we had the evening to ourselves. I was really looking forward to having some time alone with John, father and son, man to man. We picked out which movie we wanted to see and started to get ready to go. About a half hour before we needed to be in the car, the phone rang.

"I'll get it!" John yelled, making a grab for the receiver. I watched him talk quietly into the phone, turning away from me.

"Just a minute," he said into the phone. "Dad, it's Kurt. He wants me to go to a movie with him tonight." His eyes held a hopeful look.

"But John, we were going to go." I couldn't keep the disappointment out of my voice.

"I know we were, Dad," John replied, "but I'd rather go with Kurt."

* * * * *

Dependent Child to Independent Adult

The adolescent years are a time of separation. A friend once told me, with tears welling up in his eyes, "You spend so much time helping your children grow up and then you have to give them away!" During these years, they actively seek independence, yet they still need a home, food, clothing, all the necessities of life. As parents, you still wish to give guidance and direction, as you have all along. You actively seek to help them avoid the mistakes you made.

At the same time, your teenager will be looking not to you, but to themselves and friends for the answers they seek. You may find yourself "out of the loop." They are moving from dependent child to independent adult. This transition is rarely accomplished without struggle.

The Juggling Act

The teenage years can be very confusing for both teen and parent. One parent may say, "You can't do that! You're not old enough!" The other may turn around and say, "Grow up! Act your age!" Sometimes, the same parent will say both!

During these years, your teen may want to impose a double-standard. They may want all of the priviledges of an adult with only the responsibilities of a child. It makes sense to them, they feel like both, they act like both.

As they "try on" their new adult feelings, the desire for independence will grow. Your teen will probably call it "freedom!" They will demand more and more autonomy from your influence, while retaining the right to come "running home to Dad,or Mom" if things don't turn out exactly as planned.

This is why the teenage years are often called, to use the words of Charles Dickens, "... the best of times, the worst of times."

SIGNS OF A TEENAGER IN THE HOUSE

1. Physical Changes-The dread "puberty!"

2. Social Changes-From Lace to Leather

3. Emotional Changes-The Attack of the Hormones

4. Spiritual Changes-Taking Charge of Their Faith

The Physical Changes

All of us have been through this, so I don't think I need to go into the changes in detail. Suffice it to say, your child will rapidly change into a physical adult. Their sexual reproductive systems mature and boys will experience a growth spurt. They'll become taller, gangly, clumsy. Some of the shorter boys will catch up to girls who were taller in grade school.

Girls will develop "a figure." For some of you, it may be quite difficult to witness the transition from "Daddy's little girl," to sexually attractive teen. There's nothing you can do to stop it, nor should you want to.

If you think the middle school years are trying, turn it up a notch with high school *daze*. What began as a trend in middle school becomes full-blown in high school.

Teens don't always feel comfortable talking about what is happening to them physically. The emergence of their sexual nature can be difficult for both of you to acknowledge. That is why keeping the lines of communication open is so important. You won't be able to dictate whether or not your teen comes to you to talk, you can only be available when they do. If you have developed a pattern of open communication during their growing up, it will be that much easier for them to come to you, now.

Things To Watch Out For: Sexual Promiscuity

The obvious thing to watch out for, as your teen matures physically, is sexual activity. Today, over 80% of boys and 55% of girls who graduate from high school will already have engaged in sex.[1]

Virgin is not a word well thought of, in our society today. There is immense pressure on teens to become sexually active as soon as physically possible. Even with this influence from society, I believe the pendulum on sexual promiscuity may be swinging back towards abstinence.

With the onset of the AIDS virus, casual sex has lost some of its appeal. Sexually transmitted diseases have always been around, but AIDS brought the very real specter of death into sexual intimacy. While teens have been resistant to curb their sexual activity, many are heeding the warnings given to them.

Because of this, I see a revival in the concept of abstinence. Students, many of whom are Christians, are signing "Abstinence Pledges." These young people are committing to remain sexually pure until marriage. What a marvelous commitment! I wish for every young person to find the courage to sign this pledge!

The Social Changes

As your teen moves through the middle school years, not only will they develop an interest in the opposite sex, they'll also become attached to friends of the same sex. These will be their buddies, the ones they turn to for acceptance and validation.

As I learned with John, they will often choose time with their friends over time with you. It hurt for John to say he'd rather spend time with his friend than with me.

But I also knew I couldn't take it personally. I had to filter his actions through his stage in life.

Both boys and girls become more aware of their appearance during this time, and the effect their appearance has on others. Girls will begin to wear make-up and boys will actually want to shower and comb their hair!

Of course, on the opposite end, your teen may show complete distain for physical appearance. Choosing to be "themselves" by wearing baggy, unkempt clothing or brandishing a bizarre hairstyle may be their way of declaring "independence" not only from you, but from peers. This trend needs to be monitored carefully to make sure it doesn't degenerate into truly anti-social behavior.

High-schoolers, especially, will move in and out of social circles. As they try to hone in on their identity, they may try the "fit" in different groups. By their senior year in high school, though, they will have developed close friendships with two or three others. Most of their social time will be with these friends, even though they may be acquainted with many others. These special friends will have enormous influence over the decisions your teen makes. It is important, then, for these friends to be chosen wisely.

Things To Watch Out For: Inappropriate Friendships

You may or may not like your teen's choice of friends. Whether or not you approve, they will choose. Your criticism of those choices can bring division, pushing your teenager farther away from you and closer to the friend you disapprove of. So how do you communicate your reservations about their choice of friends, without causing irreparable harm to your relationship with your teen?

First, get to know more about your teen's friend. Impressions made are not always accurate. Try asking other parents about this teenager. Find out what sort of "reputation" they have in the school community. If your teen knows this friend through a specific class or activity at school, try to become involved. You'll be able to observe your teen, their friend, and the way they interact together.

Invite your teen's friend over to your house for dinner or to be with your teen. Observe your teen's reactions being around both you and their friend. If they are open and comfortable, you may be over-reacting. However, if your teen appears skittish and secretive with their friend, choosing to totally remove themselves from the normal, family environment, you may want to approach your teen.

You might start by saying, "I've been thinking about your friend and I'd like to share something with you. I know you need to be able to choose your own friends, and I want you to do that, but I'm not so sure about the friend you brought over the other night.

"Somehow, something wasn't right. I didn't feel good about the way you were acting around them. I just wonder if you both are heading in the same direction. What can you tell me about them?"

No matter how you word it, this will be delicate. It is very important you don't criticize your child for their choices, or judge their friend too harshly.

Let your teen know where you stand. Then leave the friendship decision to them: it is, anyway. Allow your teen time to think about what you've said. Pray for God's peace and Spirit to make things right. Often the undesirable friendship will drift away.

If it does not, you may need to limit the time and opportunities for your teen and this friend to be together. Try to make sure they are supervised in some way, at all times. With these types of restrictions, the friendship may falter.

As a very last resort, terminating the association may be necessary. You probably won't be able to terminate the friendship, but you can severely limit the time together. This option is unpleasant for both you and your teen. Remember, however, you are still the adult and your experience and wisdom are greater than your teen's. Just because they are moving toward adulthood doesn't mean they're there, yet.

The destructive influence of inappropriate friends can be extremely difficult to reverse. It is your job, as father, to step in when your teen's choices are causing serious damage to their life.

The Emotional Changes

Emotionally, these teenage years can be hard on adolescents. The emotions they experience - - anger, frustration, excitement, confusion - - aren't foreign to them. They will have experienced all of these before. But during the teenage years, these emotions intensify. The onslaught of emotional depth can be difficult for both of you to handle.

So many factors affect their emotional state: they worry about how they are perceived by others, how attractive they are to the opposite sex, how peers will respond to them. They constantly compare themselves to others, usually with unfavorable results.

Their emotional rollercoasters are unavoidable. The best you can hope to do is enjoy the straight-aways and hang on tight during the clickety-clackety climbs and falls! With their emotional states being unstable, you need to be their anchor. In the midst of an uncertain world, young adolescents find security and emotional stability through you.

While they may pull away from you socially, you need to be there for them, emotionally. Their feelings will both soar and be crushed by seemingly trivial events. Being available for them to talk, and to really listen to them, is important. Give them positive affirmation during this time. Remember to hug. Surprise them with small gestures. Be ready to take advantage of time together, with lots of encouragement.

The urgency of taking care of your child's physical needs will have lessened as they grow older, but when they reach adolescence, they will urgently need you to be there for them emotionally.

Things to Watch Out For: Staying Too Long in the Pit

The emotional state of teens will vary greatly. If it stays stuck too long in a "dip," you may need to intervene. A teen who withdraws from life, friends and activities, who retreats into their room, always wanting to be alone, is one who needs watching.

The problems associated with growing up can overwhelm any teen. In most, their natural excitement should surface after time. While they are experiencing many bewildering changes, the teen years should also be an exciting time of discovery. If your teen spends too much time being bewildered, and not enough time being excited, make sure to encourage a dialogue with them. Communicate your concern and seek their response. Teens don't always respond as much as parents would like, but don't give up. Look for the unexpected, teachable moments when you can reach through those teen barriers and impact your child.

Encourage your teen to participate in activities at home, school, church or even to get a job. Expect them to help out around the house, allow them to feel useful and contribute to the family. All of us need to know we have purpose and your teen is no different.

Help your child to have a sense of direction during these years. Idle time for teens is an invitation for inappropriate behavior and a sense of futility. Mike Yaconelli, of *Youth Specialties*, sees it this way: "A characteristic of kids today is what I call a paralyzed will. It frightens me that most kids have no understanding of how powerful their will is.

"On Wednesday night, I can ask a group of kids what they're going to do on Friday night. They don't know. Friday night comes, and they hear about a party. They go to it. There's booze there, so they drink it. The point is, they never decided to spend their weekend that way.

"Kids don't choose to go out and end up where they do. It's more like a cow who nibbles at a patch of grass here and then there. Pretty soon she's eating grass by a hole in the fence and later finds herself outside of it. In a while, she's lost and can't get back into the pasture.

"I honestly believe our kids are sort of nibbling their way to lostness. It's vital that we help them rediscover the value of making choices."[2]

When our children spend too much time feeling lost, they've spent too much time in the pit.

The Spiritual Changes

Spiritually, your teenager is also changing. If your family attends church, they may differ from your routine. In order to show their independence, they may suddenly dislike the teen group at church, choose to go to another church, or become increasingly active in their own teen group. All of these are an attempt to come to their own opinion about God and their spiritual nature.

During junior high, your teen may decide church isn't "cool." They resist attempts to go to class or youth group. You may find yourself arguing, cajoling or outright threatening them to go to church with the family. Persistence on your part is necessary. While you cannot force them into a spiritual relationship, you can reiterate your family rules and those activities you have decided, as head of the family, to be important for the entire family.

One compromise for you may be to allow your teen to attend a different church or teen group. Of course, you will want to check out what that group is teaching, but if the substance is sound, allow them the independence to explore their spirituality elsewhere. If you have planted spiritual seeds of your own in your children, God may have someone else in mind to do the watering for a while.

Sometimes, teens will blossom spiritually and become increasingly active at church. This may be due to their spiritual search, the other teens in the group, or an affinity with the youth leader. Whatever the reason, be as encouraging and supportive of their going to functions as you can. So much spiritual work is done during these times, use all opportunities.

Children are spiritual beings and will seek out answers to spiritual questions they have. If your family does not attend a religious organization, your teen may seek one out. Many a teenager has found faith through a para-church organization, such as *Young Life, Campus Life* or others. Much of my life has been dedicated to helping young people in their spiritual search. Often, they are looking for someone outside the family who can provide a spiritual dimension.

Whichever path they decide to take, the key is it's their path. Trust your child, trust the Lord, trust yourself and your teaching. And pray alot.

"Train a child in the way he should go, and when he is old he will not turn from it." (Proverbs 22:6 NIV) Trust the seeds you have planted to bring forth fruit later in the life of your teen.

Things to Watch Out For: Religious Cults

A teen on a spiritual search can be vulnerable to unscrupulous religious charlatans who seek not to enlighten your child, but exploit them. If your child becomes involved with a different religious group than the rest of the family, take time to investigate. Do this early. Most cults use a method of separating victims from their families by degrading family bonds. Waiting too long could literally be acting too late.

Most religious groups in the country, especially established, mainstream churches, are not cults. If you are unfamiliar with the practices of a specific group, ask questions of the leader or pastor. Go to the library and read about them. Go to your own church and ask a leader what they know about the other group.

The Separation Process

As your teenager grows physically, socially, emotionally and spiritually, they are "separating" from you. Their job, at this time, is to learn how to live as an adult without actually being one. For some parents and teens, it isn't so much a "trial-run" as it is a "run-in" with each other.

If this separation process is not handled well by both teen and parent, harm to the relationship can occur which may take years to repair, if at all. I've developed a chart to show how this decline in relationship occurs. (See end of chapter.)

As the teenager becomes more independent, they're around the house less. When they are at home, they may be unmotivated and appear "lazy." As a parent, you see the child as rebellious. Your teen will see you as too "restrictive."

If you do not deal with these feelings, you may become critical and suspicious of your teen while they are increasingly disobedient as they search for "freedom" from you. Freedom from you can be coupled with association of "undesirable" friends and a sense of drifting through life.

Drifting leads to isolation, despair and possibly, thoughts of suicide. Fathers, if you sense this downward spiral in your teenager, seek professional help for the whole family. This trend is serious and potentially life-threatening to your child.

The Light At The End Of The Tunnel

Not all teenagers end up struggling at this level. Most are delightful to be with and provide a constant enthusiasm for what they are learning and experiencing. You may not have felt like laughing during your own adolescence, but sometimes teens can be humorous. Erma Bombeck relates this story:

A woman in Illinois has a son who is "into weight-lifting.'" She noted that the stronger the muscles become in his upper arms, the weaker the muscles become in his fingers.

In other words, the boy can press his own weight, but he can't turn off a water faucet.

The answer is a simple one. Teenagers develop only one part of their bodies at a time. If they are making good grades, don't expect them to clean up their room. If you want them to have eight hours sleep a night, they can't handle the garbage. If you want the truth out of them, don't push them to turn off the lights in their room.

We have all lived through the years of parental innocence. I had a son who played basketball four hours a day. Those legs carried him back and forth on that gym floor a 100 times a day. The walking muscles that would trasnport him home on foot have not developed today....

To understand teenagers, you must understand their anatomy. No two things work at the same time.

On the eve of their 16th birthday, their hands will form little fists in anticipation of car keys which dangle from them every minute.

These same fingers cannot replace a towel on a rack.

By the time a teen is 17, there are few things that are "operational." The hearing is gone. The voice is never used. There is no sign he or she recognizes anyone. The muscles throughout the body are a mass of inertia.

The only thing that really works is the mind. It accelerates to age 35 and holds there until he or she is 35. Then it goes back to down to 17.

The eyes that develop x-ray vision to see a piece of pound cake wrapped in foil in the back of the refrigerator, will not see a dog that is tunneling under the door in an effort to relieve itself."

What's a parent to do?

Living Successfully With Your Teen

We can all identify with some aspect of Erma Bombeck's article. The trick is to be able to live through these experiences with as few scars as possible. The following suggestions should help.

1. *Don't beat yourself up when you make a mistake.*

I have yet to meet the perfect parent. Even God had family problems. "I reared children and brought them up, but they rebelled against me." (Isaiah 1:2 NIV)

We need to live with the fact we're not perfect. We're going to make mistakes. Good parenting techniques can help us cut down on the number and severity of our mistakes, not eliminate them altogether.

2. *Teens are "works in progress."*

In an instant world, building lives takes time. The coffee may be instant, the breakfast, or the replay, as well, but there are no instant relationships. Molding our children takes time and perserverence.

159

"This is the word that came to Jeremiah from the Lord: 'Go down to the potter's house, and there I will give you a message.' So I went down to the potter's house, and I saw him working at the wheel. But the pot he was shaping from the clay was marred in his hands; so the potter formed another pot, shaping it as seemed best to him.

"The word of the Lord came to me: 'O house of Israel, can I not do with you as this potter does?' declares the Lord. 'Like clay in the hand of the potter, so are you in my hand, O house of Israel.'" (Jeremiah 18:1-6 NIV)

God is at work in our lives and in the lives of our children, especially during adolescence. The rough edges are being chipped away and polished.

3. *Don't take it personally if you're not always included in your teen's life.*

They are learning to become independent from you. The only way they can do this, is to be separate. Monitor the "separation process," but don't take it personal. Teenagers need space to grow and opportunities to experience their independence.

4. *Strive for good communication.*

Actively seek communication with your teen. If you wait for them to initiate conversation, you may be waiting a long time.

Communication doesn't mean lecturing your teen all of the time. You must be prepared to listen. Decode their feelings along with their words and seek to develop a deeper level of communication. Even though they are pulling away from you, they'll know you still care and are there for them, when they need it.

Building the bridges of friendship with our children early in their lives will reap a reward, now. Remember the Equation: Rules - Relationship = Rebellion! Instill the rules, build the relationship and cut down on the rebellion.

With each child, you only have a short span of time to be the father your children need. Your teenager is growing up and will soon be an adult. Choose wisely, Dad, and your family will reap the benefits for generations to come.

THE BOTTOM LINE

When you're on a roller-coaster, the best thing to do is just hang on, and enjoy the ride!

1. As a teenager, can you remember a "best time" and a "worst time" with your father?

2. What was the one thing about you back then, that irritated your parents the most?

3. When you were a teenager, what did you appreciate most about your parents?

4. If you have teenagers now, what is the one thing you wish they'd do differently?

5. What are you doing to encourage your teen?

I Just Can't Talk to You Anymore!
Communciation Breakdown
Between Teen and Parent

Teen.......

Shows more independence.

Shows lack of cooperation, laziness.

Is ungrateful toward parent. Becomes more rebellious of authority.

Begins to openly disobey. Chooses to stay out late. Starts to bad-mouth parents to friends.

Recedes into their own world. Parents aren't let in on anything. Rebellion takes the form of sexual promiscuity, inappropriate music, pornography.

"I can't wait until I'm 18! Then, I'm moving out!"

Experiences isolation from the rest of the family. Wonders if anyone cares. Friends have their own problems and are unresponsive. Experiences guilt, despair and depression. Has thoughts of suicide.

Parent......

Requests help around the house. Figures the teen is "old enough" to help.

Demands help at home. Usually in a loud, assertive voice.

Begins to criticize activity choices and choice of friends.

Becomes suspicious of teen. Constantly questions teen about companions and activities.

Threatens their teen. Restrictions, being grounded, loss of priviledges, even threats of being kicked-out of the home.

Gives up on ever understanding their child. Quits trying to help or improve relationship.

Inwardly grieves the loss of relationship.

Chapter Thirteen......DAD THE COMMUNICATOR

How Can I Be A Better Dad?

MEMORANDUM
FROM: YOUR CHILD
TO: DAD

Don't spoil me.
I know quite well I shouldn't have everything I ask for.

Don't be afraid to be firm with me.
I need to know where the boundaries are.

Don't use force with me.
All I learn is that power counts.

Be consistent.
*Otherwise, I get confused. I'll try to
get "away" with whatever I can.*

Don't make me feel smaller than I am.
I'll just try to be "a big shot."

Let me do things for myself.
Doing everything for me makes me
feel like a baby, and I'll act like one.

Correct me in private.
My brain stops working when I'm embarassed.

Let me make mistakes.
I learn from those experiences.

Answer my honest questions.
I can always get the answer somewhere else.

Apologize to me when you make a mistake.
I might actually forgive you.

Treat me like you treat your friends.
I'd like to be your friend, too.[1]

Taking A Risk

Fathers, you usually believe you know what your children need. You figure you've got a pretty good idea what it takes to be Dad. You know how you were raised. You've talked to your buddies at work or at church. How about taking a step into the unknown? How about taking a risk and going directly to the source?

"What can I do to be a good father for you?"

It's risky. Kids usually answer these types of questions with more than a grunt or shrug. Their response can contain valuable information.

As I go about, giving seminars and teaching, I encourage fathers to ask their children this question. Later, I try to go back and find out what the responses were. Too often, when I ask them how their discussion went, they tell me they never seemed to get around to asking the question!

We stand at the threshold of a deeper relationship with our children, yet are afraid to take the step. In so many aspects of our life, we can be take-charge leaders. Many of you are competent, confident business leaders, supervisors, diligent workers. You are leaders at work, at church and in the community. You're even responsible family men, but you shy away from being really close, really open, with your children.

The window-of-opportunity available for you to develop a close friendship with your children closes a little with each passing day. Avoid the question, hope for the best, and you may find yourself with a distant and stormy relationship with your growing child.

Take the risk, ask the question, respond to the answer, and you can look forward to a close relationship that will carry into adulthood.

Fear Of The Unknown

Most men like things to be "under control." You may not have realized it, but your total control over your life ended when you had children. Their unpredictability has a way of throwing even the most carefully constructed schedule into the wastebasket. The most control you can hope to have is over yourself. So much of your joint environment with your children will be out of your control. The sleep you needed before the big presentation can evaporate with an ear infection at three in the morning. The afternoon set aside for painting the basement, and getting it finished, can never be a reality, thanks to "little helpers."

Asking your children questions means giving up control. You can be in control all the way through the question. Your control ends when their answer begins. The ball is in their court. What will they say? How will they react? This fear of the unknown is what keeps many men from having a serious discussion with their children. Here are a few suggestions:

1. Arrange the time and place. Try taking your child to breakfast or lunch on "neutral ground." Be sure to leave enough time for discussion.

2. Don't just start off with the "big question." Begin with an introductory dialogue. Make sure your questions aren't ones that have one word answers, like, "How are you doing?"............. "Fine." Try one like, "What's the funniest thing you remember when you were younger?"

3. Get around to asking the "big question." "You know, I've been thinking about how I'm doing as your dad. I really want to be a good one, but I could use your help. What can I do to be a better dad to you?"

Conversation Killers

Come Quickly to Your Defense.
The quicker you become defensive, the quicker the discussion will end.

You asked them to share and they did. Look where it got them. If you feel defensive, try saying, "I didn't realize you felt that way." The key is to listen, not defend.

Take What You've Learned And Do Nothing.
You have an obligation to take what you hear from your child and respond. The things your child tells you are very important to them. Show they are important to you by acting upon them.

Keys To Being A Good Dad

Once the lines of communication are open, the way you respond will determine if they remain so. If your children are small or timid, you may not get all the answers you need on what to do to be a better father for your children. Here are some characteristics I've found to be helpful, gathered from my years counseling fathers and being a father and step-father.

Many of these characteristics are actions, not words. But your actions will communicate to your child in a loud voice. Work to keep the lines of communication open with your children and let your actions keep them open.

1. Be a leader, not a dictator. Be someone who takes charge of the situation, not someone who charges over others. Children need to see you in the lead at home. This gives them a sense of security.

Your leadership can include everything from fixing a toy, to coaching their ball team, to leading prayers at meal and bedtimes. In each instance, you are showing you care enough to take the initiative, to be involved in all aspects of their lives.

This will communicate
you are interested in them.

2. Empathize with your children. Be excited when they are excited, even if it is over the seventy-eighth "most beautiful rock in the world!" Hold them when they're hurting.

This will communicate
they are not alone in the world.

3. Show them about life by how you live yours. How do you handle disappointment? By sulking and pouting? How do you handle being angry? By hitting a wall or yelling and screaming? How do you

167

deal with problems? Do you talk about them and attempt to find a solution. Children need to see how you handle life's ups and downs.

This will communicate how to be an adult.

4. Show them how to handle success. Do you gloat or brag about your accomplishments? Do you have an inflated opinion of yourself? Kids usually reach a point where they see through this. Very few people accomplish life's great successes totally on their own. By showing gratitude for the work of others and thankfulness for the results, success is put into its correct context.

This will communicate the value of humility.

5. Don't neglect discipline. Children want to know their limits. There is great freedom in having the boundaries clearly marked. When children wonder, they worry. Remember chapter nine. Discipline your children to ensure they learn the lessons they'll need to survive as healthy adults.

This will communicate
your love and care for them.

More Time With Dad

I would be willing to bet the overwhelming answer to the question, "What can I do to be good dad to you?" would be answered with, "Spend more time with me." I hope you are willing to risk and ask the question.

And I hope you're willing to respond to the answer. When I have asked the question of children over the years, "What could your father have done to be a better dad?" this answer always comes up. They rarely think of things they wanted, but didn't get. What they longed for was the companionship of the most important man in their lives, their father.

Their answer may be just that simple. What do they want? They want more of you. This poem, entitled, *"Give Him A Day,"* sums it up:

> *What shall you give to one small boy?*
> *A glamorous game, a tinseled toy?*
> *A Boy Scout knife, a puzzle pack?*
> *A train that runs on some curving track?*
> *A picture book, a real live pet?*
> *No, there's plenty of time for such things yet.*
> *Give him a day for his very own.*
> *Just one small boy and his dad alone.*
> *A walk in the woods, a romp in the park.*
> *A fishing trip from dawn until dark.*
> *Give him a gift that only you can,*
> *The companionship of his "old man."*
> *Games are outgrown and toys decay.*
> *But he'll never forget,*
> *If you give him a day.*[2]

THE BOTTOM LINE

Ask the question and honor the answer.

1. Did your father ever ask you the "big question?"
   How did you, or would you, respond?

2. How do you think your child would respond to this question?

3. What would be a good time and place to ask your child this question?

4. What fears are holding you back from asking?

5. How important will it be for your child to know you want to be a better dad?

Chapter Fourteen......DAD THE ACCOUNTABLE

Fathering Through Accountability

Ever play hide-and-seek with your young child? It probably went something like this:

Off your child went to hide, giggling loudly. She chose the closest place she could find and scrunched down, eyes wide.

"I wonder where Annie is?" you said, tip-toeing down the hall. "I know she's around here somewhere!"

In her little hiding place, Annie could barely contain herself. The game is called hide-and-seek, but Annie desperately wanted to be found. She waited patiently, tucked up, until she couldn't take it anymore. "Here I am!" she cried, finally, running into your arms.

* * * * *

Annie wanted very much to be found. She made sure she was. It's just no fun for a child to stay hidden. It's not much fun for an adult, but a lot of us spend a great deal of time hiding from ourselves, our peers, and our God.

Confessing vs. Concealing

"He who conceals his transgressions will not prosper, but he who confesses and forsakes them will obtain mercy." (Proverbs 28:13 RSV)

What we know as children, we often have to re-learn as adults. Most children start out as terrible liars. They just aren't good at concealing the truth. Their eyes wander, they hem and haw, their feet shuffle. Usually, they end up blurting out the truth without much pressure at all. They "confess" freely they broke the lamp or cut off the cats whiskers or let the hamster out of the cage.

The older we get, the more uncomfortable we are with confessing, the more adept we become at concealing. We have the "public mask" and the "private face." The more we conceal and the less we confess, the farther apart those two become. This dichotomy of public vs. private is damaging to all our relationships.

The High Price Of Hiding From Self

Concealing the truth about ourselves causes us to live out a lie. The tension produced from living this lie damages our physical bodies. Extra stress occurs when our conscience is not clean, when we are battling the ghost of past wrongs. Sir Walter Scott put it best when he said, "Oh what a tangled web we weave when first we practice to deceive."

Deception is time and energy consuming. We get worn out mentally trying to keep the lid on our lies. We get worn out emotionally using up energy to stay hidden from others, not to let our feelings show. We get worn out physically through anxiety and stress.

David wrote in the Psalms, "When I declared not my sin, my body wasted away." (Psalms 32:3 RSV) "There is no soundness in my flesh because of Thy indignation; there is no health in my bones because of my sin. For my iniquities have gone over my head; they weigh like a burden too heavy for me." (Psalm 3:3-4 RSV)

Our bodies know when something isn't right. We become troubled, anxious and worried. Yet, we strive to maintain the illusion nothing is wrong.

The High Price Of Hiding From Others

Bruce Larson is his book, *No Longer Strangers,* says, "Men think they should appear objective and tough, striving, achieving and unsentimental. And above all, unexpressive of the person inside. They are never, of course, to show weakness, and if a man shows his feelings he is afraid that will be regarded as inferior to his fellows. Therefore, he is obligated to hide much of his real self."[1] Though we wear a mask of respectability, of invulnerability, we cannot escape the price of concealment.

There is a bonding, a camaraderie, which results when men share their true selves. If those around us are only allowed to view our successes, walls of jealousy, envy and divisiveness are built. Bridges of friendship come from revealing our difficulties, failures and fears.

The High Price Of Hiding From God

Hiding from God is really a useless endeavor. David, again, in Psalms says:

"Where can I go from your Spirit? Where can I flee from your presence? If I go up to the heavens, you are there; if I make my bed in the depths, you are there. If I rise on the wings of the dawn, if I settle on the far side of the sea, even there your hand will guide me, your right hand will hold me fast. If I say, 'Surely the darkness will hide me and the light become night around me,' even the darkness will not be dark to you; the night will shine like the day, for darkness is as light to you."[2]

The high price we pay for attempting to deceive God is damage to our souls. And it is without reason, for God already knows what we're dying to conceal! Like most of us, He desires honesty in our relationship with Him. He wants us to be strong enough to admit our mistakes, confessing our sin, and work toward doing better.

In 1 John 1:9, there is a promise: "If we confess our sins, He is faithful and just, and will forgive our sins and cleanse us from all unrighteousness." (RSV)

How many times have you, as a father, faced a child who made a mistake. You know the truth about what happened. You can see the broken window or the crushed plant or the ruined dress shoes. You don't need to be omniscient to realize the truth.

"Billy, what happened to the _____?" you ask.

Now, you're not really asking because you don't know. You're asking to gain your child's version of events and enable your child to admit their mistake. Often, you are more upset at their attempts to lie and deceive you, than you are about the window or the plant or the shoes. Those are just objects. You care more about the heart of your child.

If you've felt that way, you're not alone. So has God. In Genesis, God asks one of those *I-already-know-the-answer* questions: "Then the man and his wife heard the sound of the Lord God as he was walking in the garden in the cool of the day, but they hid from the Lord God among the trees of the garden.

"But the Lord God called to the man, 'Where are you?'

"He answered, 'I heard you in the garden, and I was afraid because I was naked; so I hid.'" (Genesis 3:8-10 NIV)

God knew perfectly well where Adam was. The questions was asked so Adam would have to confront his sin. Why? So lightning bolts could reign down from the sky and burn him to a crisp? No, so Adam would realize his sin, confess and ask forgiveness.

When we try to hide our true selves from God, not only is it an exercise in futility, it damages the most vital relationship we have: the one with our Father in heaven.

Overcoming Hidden Sin

1. Be accountable for your sin before God.

"Search me, O God, and know my heart; test me and know my thoughts. See if there is any offensive way in me..." (Psalm 139:23-24 NIV)

Ask God to help you root out the secrets you've been hiding. He knows just where they are and you may have forgotten where you hid them.

Once you have acknowledged your sin, become accountable for it. Accept your sinfulness and ask forgiveness. David in Psalm 51 was not afraid to do just that: "...according to your great compassion, blot out my transgressions. Wash away all my iniquity and cleanse me from my sin. For I know my transgressions, and my sin is ever before me. Against you, you only, have I sinned and done what is evil in your sight...Create in me a clean heart, O God, and renew a steadfast spirit within me...Restore to me the joy of your salvation and grant me a willing spirit, to sustain me." (Psalm 51:1-4,10-12 NIV) That about says it all.

2. Be accountable for your sin before others.

If there is a need to ask forgiveness for a wrong you've committed, no matter how far in the past, seek out that person and attempt to make it right. This won't be easy, but choosing to remove the sinful secrets from your life will bring inner peace and removal of guilt.

3. Live your life accountable to others.

One way to guard yourself against sin gaining a foothold in secret is to align yourself with peers who will keep you accountable. Over the years, I have met with a group of men who are dedicated to holding each other accountable for the way we live our lives. Their example, encouragement, and insight has been a tremendous help in my life.

Accountability Is Not A Bad Word

"As iron sharpens iron, so one man sharpens another." (Proverbs 27:17 NIV)

"A Christian man who is not in a small group is an accident waiting to happen." *Dr. Howard Hendricks.*

When you are accountable to another person, you are simply asking them to help you. You're admitting you need their encouragment to follow through on important things in life. Within a small group, each man can not only encourage the other, but motivate each to live according to joint principles.

In the early days of space exploration, rocket launches were common. They would occur off launching pads in Florida and travel down the Atlantic Ocean. Most would fly according to their flight plan. Some had to be destroyed in flight because they deviated from their flight plan and couldn't be corrected. If they weren't destroyed immediately, the initial deviation could lead to greater and greater straying from the correct path.

We can be like that. We have slight deviations in our lives. Accountability points out the correct path for us. Like the rocket, what starts out as a slight deviation can end up a major departure from the right path. It is imperative our deviations, our sins, are detected early and corrected. Sometimes, we can do that for ourselves and other times, we need the gentle correction of good friends to whom we've made ourselves accountable.

Accountability is not a bad word. It is for our benefit and ultimate good. True friends are those who hold our best interest at heart, and us accountable.

Faithful Friends

For fifteen years, I have met with a group of faithful friends. Together we have weathered divorce, financial difficulties, kid problems, remarriage, moves, being fired, job searches, death of loved ones. We've taken vacations together, gotten together to ring in the New Year, spent endless hours over lunch, and generally had a wonderful time being together and sharing our lives. I cannot adequately explain to you what a blessing these men have been in my life. And what a blessing it has been to be a part of their lives.

The caring we have for each other goes deep to the heart. If I should need any of them, one or all would be on my doorstep within an hour. They know I would do the same.

We didn't start out that way. Our group began as a way to get to know each other more deeply, to help each other live our lives as men successfully. Time was the key to building the trust necessary to develop our lasting friendships.

The longer we were together, the more transparent we became. We dropped masks and shields, one by one, until we allowed ourselves to be vulnerable to the group. Over time, we knit and bonded together. Trust grew. Friendship deepened.

If you feel you would benefit from meeting regularly with a group of men, why not consider starting an accountability group of your own? For a group such as this to function well, there are a set of ground rules, or principles, I have found beneficial, which govern participation.

In essense, each member of a group is entering into a covenant with each other, not unlike Jonathan and David. (1 Samuel 18-20) Following is a list of eight principles of covenant groups.[3] If you form a group, I encourage you to utilize these principles. If you look for an existing group to join, I urge you to find one who practices these principles. Such a group will be of great benefit to you.

Covenant Principles

1. *The Covenant of Affirmation*
There is nothing you have done, or will do, to make me stop loving you. I may not agree with your actions, but I will love you as a person and do all I can to hold you up in God's affirming love.

2. *The Covenant of Confidentiality*
I promise to keep whatever is shared with the group confidential in order to allow each member to feel safe enough to share.

3. *The Covenant of Prayer*
I promise to pray for you on a regular basis, believing our caring Father desires His children to pray for one another and to ask Him for the blessings we need.

4. *The Covenant of Availability*
Anything I have - - time, energy, insight, possessions - - are at your disposal, if you should need them. I give these to you as a priority in my life. I promise to be available for us to meet together regularly.

5. *The Covenant of Openness*
I promise to be open, disclosing my feelings, struggles, joys and pain, as well as I am able. I cannot make it in life without you. I trust you with my needs. I need you.

6. *The Covenant of Sensitivity*
Even as I desire to be known and understood by you, I promise to be sensitive to you and your needs to the best of my ability.

7. *The Covenant of Honesty*

I promise to trust our relationship enough to be honest about what I feel and what I hear from you. I promise to speak the truth, in love.

8. *The Covenant of Accountability*

I consider my God-given gifts available to be used for the common good. If I discover areas of myself I am not using as God intended, I promise to ask your help in being accountable to God and to you for becoming more fully who God designed me to be.

By participating in a small group of accountable men, we can benefit ourselves, our spouse, and our children. All of us need care and loving concern. We need affirmation and encouragement. We need to be accountable to others for our actions. Each of these needs can be addressed in an accountability group.

None of us is immune to evil. 1 Peter 5:8-9 (NIV) warns, "Be self-controlled and alert. Your enemy the devil prowls around like a roaring lion looking for someone to devour. Resist him, standing firm in the faith, because you know that your brothers... are undergoing the same kind of suffering."

Fathering Through Accountability

A burning coal, if taken from the fire and left alone on the hearth, soon dies out. But if that same coal is left with others, it continues to burn and glow. Likewise, in our fathering, it is difficult to "go it alone." Surrounded by other fathers, we feed off each other. We keep each other sharpened and motivated.

An accountability group will help you follow through with your plans to be a good father for your children. They can suggest ways to better utilize your time with spouse and children. Many of them will be working on the same struggles you are. Two heads really are better than one. Put them together to come up with solutions to your parenting problems.

Allow the men in your group to really get to know you. Show them your inner self and trust them to respond with love and forgiveness. Be prepared to forgive, when they fall short. This life we live can be tough, but a burden shared is a burden lessened.

THE BOTTOM LINE

*We are accountable to someone for
the life we live whether we choose
to acknowledge it or not.*

1. Why is it uncomfortable for some men
    to speak honestly to other men about
    problems in their life?

2. Who do you talk to about the struggles
    you're having?

3. Can you picture yourself becoming
    involved with an accountability group of
    men? Why? Why not?

4. What expectations would you have of
    such a group?

5. What would need to happen for you to
    become part of an accountability group?

Chapter Fifteen......DAD THE DO-ER

Entering the Arena with Confidence

The moment you commit yourself, the opportunity for success becomes a reality.[1]

William Shakespeare, in *Measure for Measure*, wrote, "Our doubts are traitors and make us lose the good we oft might win, by fearing to attempt."

A father's role is formidable. It demands all we have, and more. We often feel overwhelmed, wondering if we're making any progress. We doubt and so we don't do.

I'm reminded of a story I heard about two moose hunters in Alaska. They flew into a small, pristine lake in a four-seater plane. As the pilot dropped them off with their gear, he reminded them to bag one moose only. The plane wouldn't be able to hold any more weight and still clear the trees at the end of the lake.

"I'll be back in a week to pick you up, same spot," the pilot said, over the noise of the prop.

As the two men were setting up camp, they heard the pounding of hooves along the ridge above the lake. Glancing over, they saw a huge bull moose. They grabbed their rifles and headed up the hill toward the ridge. Stalking their prey carefully, they finally had him ridge. Stalking their prey carefully, they finally had him in their cross-hairs. Together, they fired. Down went the moose. Gathering up the carcass, they drug it back to camp. With a week left to go, they had already bagged their one moose. They were still able to hike and fish for the rest of the week.

On the day the plane was to come back for them, they were breaking camp and again heard the sound of hooves above them. Before long, back they came with another moose.

"How'd it go?" the pilot asked, after landing the plane on the lake.

"Terrific!" they shouted, showing the pilot two kills.

"I don't know about taking them both back," the pilot said, skeptical.

"Oh, come on," the two men pleaded. "We did it last year!"

"Okay, but we'll have to pack everything carefully," he said, relenting.

No sooner had they cleared the end of the lake when one of the pontoons caught on the top of the forest. Down went the plane, breaking apart as it crashed through the trees. Camping gear, plane parts, moose meat went everywhere.

The men were dazed, but still in one piece. As they were regaining consciousness, one of the hunters said to the other, "Where are we?"

Shaking out the cobwebs, the other hunter looked around and replied, "I reckon about ten feet further than we were last year at this time!"

*   *   *   *   *

Some days you may wonder if you're making any progress at all.

However you're feeling, don't give up! Your children need you to keep trying, even if it seems you only manage to be a little ways ahead.

Entering The Arena

"It's not the critic who counts, not the one who points out how the strong man stumbled or how the doer of deeds might have done them better.

"The credit belongs to the man who is actually in the arena; whose face is marred by blood and sweat and dust; who strives valiantly but errs and comes up short again and again because there is no human endeavor without shortcomings; who knows the great enthusiasms - the great devotions; and who, if he wins, knows the triumphs of high achievement and who, if his efforts are checkered by defeat, at least fails while daring greatly; so that his place shall never be with those cold and timid souls who know neither victory nor defeat." *Teddy Roosevelt*

Three Types of Fathers

Within our society, there are three types of fathers: those who make things happen, those who watch things happen, and those who wonder, "What happened?" The *Make It Happen Father* is actively involved in the lives of his children on a day-to-day basis. He is investing his time, energy and emotions in his children.

The *Watch It Happen Father* is physically present - emotionally absent. He leaves much of the child-rearing, bedtime stories, teaching moments, discipline, even the fun times, to Mom. He may be a good provider financially, and sees this as his duty, but chooses not to become involved with providing for his children emotionally.

The *What Happened? Father* looks back at the carnage of emotional neglect over the growing-up years and wonders how his relationship with his children could have turned out so wrong. His tendency is to blame everyone and everything else for his estrangement with his children.

My hope is for all of you who read this book, no matter what your pattern has been up to this point, to determine to be a *Make It Happen Father.*

Confidently Take Your Place

Another hope I have is for fathers not to dwell in deep guilt over past failures. I would rather all would be encouraged to take their place as a responsible father. If so, there will be a new generation of fathers who understand the significance of nurturing and raising emotionally healthy children.

Past failures don't need to be looked on as completely negative. They can be a source of learning, if you are open. For many, the past as father and child will have painful memories of unmet expectations. Now is the time to resolve to take those mistakes you experienced as a child, and made as a father, and turn them into valuable teaching lessons. In this way, you can gain control of yourself and your past.

I have always liked these statements from a veteran father. He said if he were starting his family over again, these are the things he would have done.[2] Each of us has a chance to start over with ours.

If I Could, I Would......

*Try to encourage my children *more*
*Love and value my wife *more*
*Help my children to feel they belong *more*
*Laugh with my family *more*
*Listen to feelings *more*
*Teach thankfulness to my children *more*
*Meditate on God and His Word *more*
*Share my faith with my children *more*
*Nurture my family *more*

It's Party Time!

We often celebrate new beginnings with a party. Couples have an engagement party. Weddings, the beginning of a new family, are really one big party. Expectant mothers have baby showers. How about a Fatherhood Party for an expectant Father?[3]

Invite a group of male friends to celebrate the renewed commitment to fathering. (This is a great opportunity for a father to honor a son, or son-in-law.) Invited friends are asked to bring a specific gift of wisdom, and share for a few minutes their wisdom about being a dad. Sharing might include stories, jokes, experiences about what worked and what didn't, concerns, a poem or, even, a song.

It isn't necessary to invite only fathers. Any man will have wisdom about fathers, even if it comes from being the child of one.

During your Fatherhood Party make sure to share wisdom but steer clear of offering advice. Stay away from a recitation of "You should......" Allow this time to be an encouraging, up-lifting rite-of-passage for the new Dad!

Seize The Day!

You can read all the books about swimming or golfing, but until you get into the pool or out on the golf course, you're not a swimmer or golfer. You can read all the books on fathering and family values, but unless you enter the arena, you're not using what you've learned. The choice is yours, Dad.

I urge you to enter the arena with confidence. Become involved in your child's activities. Be there through the triumphs and trials, through the hopes and dreams, through the everyday adventures of their life. If you're living away from your children, don't allow the *distance* to keep you *distant* from your children. Challenge yourself to be a do-er and not just a hear-er. Don't allow opportunites to slip by. Your children need you! Hear the heartfelt words from the song, "You Were Always On My Mind."[4]

Maybe I didn't hold you,
All those lonely, lonely times.
I guess I never told you,
I'm so happy that you're mine.
The little things I should have said and done,
But I never took the time.......

Children Rarely Remember What We Say,
Seldom Remember What We Do,
But They Will Never Forget
How We Made Them Feel...

Notes

Introduction
1 William Bennett; this quote excerpted from a speech given to The Heritage Foundation, December 7, 1993.
2 National Fatherhood Initiative; Lancaster, PA, statistical information folder; *What reduces crime, child poverty, teen pregnancy, AND requires no new taxes?* March, 1995.
3 Newsweek Magazine, August 30, 1993; as reported by the National Fatherhood Initiative.
4 Ecclesiastes 3:2 (NIV)

Chapter 1
1 Author unknown to me.
2 Ann Landers Column; name not given; Bellevue Journal American, June 2, 1988.
3 Psalm 139:13-16 (NIV).
4 Matthew 18:2, 3 (NIV)
5 Matthew 18:6 (NIV)
6 Words from "Wind Beneath My Wings", Henley-Silbar, songwriters, sung by Roger Whittaker. Manufactured and distributed by BMG Music, New York, NY.

Chapter 2
1 Mark V. Hansen, "Are You Going To Help Me?" from the book, Chicken Soup for the Soul, Jack Canfield and Mark Victor Hansen. Health Communications, Inc., Deerfield Beach, FL. p. 273-274.
2 Children Learn What They Live, author unknown to me.
3 "Just Waiting for You, Dad". Adopted from a story told at a fathering conference, by Stu Weber, author of Tender Warrior and Locking Arms, Multnomah Books.

Chapter 3
1 Sir Walter Scott, Marmion, (Canto VI, stanza 117), 1808.
2 Harry and Sandy Chapin, "Cat's in the Cradle". Copyright 1974 Story Songs, Ltd.
3 National Fatherhood Initiative, Lancaster, PA, statistical information folder; March 1995.
4 Poem, "I'd rather see a sermon....." Author unknown to me.

Chapter 4
1 Poem—Anonymous.
2 Northwest Fathering Forum Newsletter, Fall, 1994.
3 Helen Colton, The Gift of Touch: How physical contact improves communication, pleasure and health. Seaview/Putnam Publisher, New York.

Chapter 5
1 National Fatherhood Initiative, Lancaster, PA, statistical information folder; March 1985
2 Gary Smalley, If Only He Knew, Zondervan Publishing House, Grand Rapids, Michigan, P. 48.

Chapter 6
1 Dean Merrill, "Father and Daughter: Building a Legacy of Love." New Man magazine, published by Strang Communications Co., Jan/Feb, 1995. p. 26.
2 Steve Kelly, Seattle Times Sports Columnist. "Games bind fathers, kids for a lifetime". Fathers Day, 1994.
3 Ibid.
4 Poem, "Please, Just Listen". Ray Houghton, M.D. Berkeley, CA, Teen Times, Nov/Dec '79.

Chapter 7
1 National Fatherhood Initiative; Lancaster, PA, statistical information folder; What reduces crime, child poverty, teen pregnancy, AND requires no new taxes? March 1995..
2 Travis Simpkins, "Growing Up Is Hard To Do", Newsweek magazine, June 21, 1993.

Chapter 8
1 From the movie, "My Girl", Columbia TriStar Home Video, Burbank, CA.
2 Corrie Ten Boom, with John and Elizabeth Sherrill, The Hiding Place, G.K. Hall, Publisher, Boston, 1973.
3 Bruce Larson, There's a Lot More to Health Than Being Sick. Word Books, Publisher, Waco, TX. 1984, p.28.

Chapter 9
1 Carl Pickhart, Parenting the Adolescent, LCN, Inc., Publisher, 1987.
2 Gordon Dalbey, Father and Son, Thomas Nelson, Publisher, Nashville, TN, 1992.
3 Houston Police Department, unable to verify; one-page handout at fathering conference acknowledges Houston Police Department.
4 Dr. Fitshugh Dodson, *"How to Discipline Effectively"*, from the book, Experts Advise Parents, edited by Eileen Schiff, published by Delacorte Press, New York.
5 Ibid.

Chapter 11
1 Poem, "The Average Child", listed author is Mike Buscemi.

Chapter 12
1 *Implications; Taking Research Beyond Information to Application;* Center for Youth Studies, S. Hamilton, MA, Sprint, 1992, p. 7.
2 Mike Yaconelli, Youth Specialties, "Today's Whole New Kind of Kid", from an address given to Young Life leaders.

Chapter 13
1 Words taken from a Poem; "A Memo from Your Child". The reference on the handout says Blair Enterprise.
2 Poem, "Give Him a Day" Ann Landers Column, from "Ruth" in New Haven, published in Bellevue, WA Journal American.

Chapter 14
1 Bruce Larson, No Longer Strangers, Word Books, Publisher, Waco, TX, 1971, p. 87.
2 Psalm 139:7-12 (NIV).
3 "Eight principles of Covenant Groups", shared with me by Conrad Jacobsen, founder of Teleios. Telios is a non-profit ministry of small groups for men, based in Seattle, WA.

Chapter 15
1 Performance Limited Edition Lithograph, G. Neill Companies, Sunrise, FL.
2 These thoughts taken from an article entitled, "If I Were Starting My Family Again", the author is unknown to me.
3 Griggs Irvin, "Welcome to Fatherhood", used with permission from his "Welcome to Fatherhood" paper.
4 Words from "Always on My Mind", Carson-James-Christopher-Thompson, song writers, sung by Roger Whittaker. Manufactured and distributed by BMG Music, New York, NY.

ADDITIONAL COPIES ORDER FORM

MY FATHER, MY HERO:
Becoming Your Child's Best Friend

How about a gift of this book to:
A new father—An expectant father—Fathers of young children—Step-fathers—A Grandfather—Men's small groups, for discussion. Mothers will also find encouragement from this book...or think about utilizing My Father, My Hero for employment enrichment programs!

Name

Address

City   State   Zip

Phone

Check/money order enclosed payable to: Family Insights

☐ Please charge my: ☐ Visa   ☐ Master Card
                             ☐ Discover   ☐ Diners
                             ☐ American Express

card #   exp. date

signature

Quantity	Total
at $9.95* each	
postage & handling	
WA residents add 8.2% state sales tax	
Total	

* discounts for large orders available
** Canadian price is $13.95

Postage and handling
Orders up to $25.00   add $2.50
$25.01 to $50.00   add $3.50
$50.01 to $100.00   add $5.00
Above $100.00   call for amount
Call for foreign postal charges

To order by mail	To order by phone	To order by fax
Family Insights	1-800-595-4415	(206) 882-9991
17617 NE 33rd Pl.	Order by phone weekdays	
Redmond, WA 98052	from 9am-6pm Pacific Time	

Please have your credit card number ready.

For information and bookings on Family Insights', "Let's Hear It For Dad!" Seminar; or parenting seminars, conferences or retreats,

please contact Terry Olsen at (206) 881-1109.